ON DUTY IN BANGLADESH

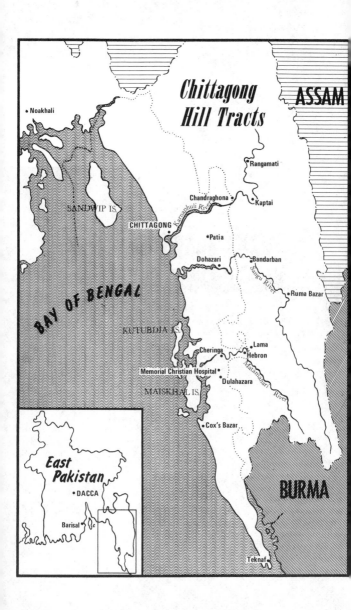

Chittagong Hill Tracts

ASSAM

• Noakhali

• Rangamati

Chandraghona
• Kaptai

SANDWIP IS.

CHITTAGONG

• Patia

• Dohazari
• Bandarban

BAY OF BENGAL

Sangu River

• Ruma Bazar

KUTUBDIA IS.

Cheringa
• Lama
Hebron

Memorial Christian Hospital •
• Dulahazara

MAISKHAL IS.

Matamahari River

• Cox's Bazar

East
Pakistan

• DACCA

Barisal

BURMA

Teknaf •

ON DUTY IN BANGLADESH

by

JEANNIE LOCKERBIE

ZONDERVAN PUBLISHING HOUSE
A DIVISION OF THE ZONDERVAN CORPORATION
GRAND RAPIDS, MICHIGAN

To the children and the young people
of Bangladesh
— with the prayer that
they will grow up knowing peace
and freedom in their homeland.

ON DUTY IN BANGLADESH
Copyright © 1973 by The Zondervan Corporation
Grand Rapids, Michigan

Library of Congress Catalog Card Number: 72-95513

Library of Congress Cataloging in Publication Data

Lockerbie, Jeannie
  On duty in bangladesh

Autobiographical.
1. Bangladesh — Politics and Government — 1971-
2. Missions, American. 3. Missions — Bangladesh.
I. Title.
DS 485. B492L63 954.9'205

Printed in the United States of America

Contents

Introduction

Nothing was further from my mind than writing a book.

The events of 1971 are too deeply etched in my mind and in my heart for me to need a personal written reminder. My reaction to the suggestion that I document these happenings was to laugh at the idea.

Where would I find the material to authenticate the memories and feelings which that year evoked? And where would I find the time to do the work involved in preparing a manuscript? With appalling need staring us in the face and crowding into our already full days! But in thinking and praying about this, I found myself reconsidering. We who had lived through those days and learned what it meant to rely on the Lord in a new way, not only for protection, but also for the supply of our needs, had a responsibility to share this living lesson with others.

Searching through desk drawers, I uncovered scribbled notes, newspaper clippings, and the notebook which I jokingly called "my journal." From these beginnings the book emerged.

Dramatic events and tragedy were not unknown to those of us living and serving in this land. In the years since I joined our missionary team in 1963, we have lived through devastating cyclones in this area that has been described as "a meteorological suction cup which beckons storms to invade the coast"; we stood helplessly by watching as our most gifted missionary-linguist died; we suffered together through a debilitating disease which resulted in having to shut down our hospital and other ministries; we ached at the disappointments and disillusionment encountered in trying to assist in the birth of the church of Christ in this area.

But the events of 1971 eclipsed all of these.

In sharing, through this book, my own experiences and the experiences of missionary colleagues and nationals (both Christian and non-Christian), my purpose is twofold:

— that great encouragement and inspiration will come to the host of men and women, boys and girls who have unfailingly upheld us by prayer and material support throughout this time

— that volumes of prayer — real "prayer without ceasing" — will be offered for this new nation of Bangladesh, for its government as they undertake mammoth reconstruction.

Multitudes have never yet heard that God loves them and is personally interested in them as individuals and that Christ died for them. Christians around the world, united in prayer, could keep the doors of officialdom open in Bangladesh so that believers of all nationalities can publish this good news.

JEANNIE LOCKERBIE
Chittagong, Bangladesh

Acknowledgments

I wish to express my appreciation to those who have contributed to this book's becoming a reality.

First, to Dr. Clyde M. Narramore, to whom the germ of an idea came while riding along a busy Los Angeles freeway. It was his, "something should be written about Bangladesh by someone who is there," that sparked such a book.

Special thanks is due to my mother, Jeanette W. Lockerbie, who encouraged me to try to capture the events, the fears, the feelings of those twelve months from December 1970 to December 1971. Having lured me into writing, she then devoted much time to editing and to correcting, as she phrased it, "your original way of spelling."

I am indebted to Dr. Donn Ketcham and to the Rev. Jay Walsh for sharing their diaries with me, thus adding insight to various situations. Others of our Association of Baptists missionary family willingly related particular incidents in which they were involved.

As a testimony to the goodness of God in preserving their lives, a number of our national believers shared their traumatic experiences during the days of horror and tragedy.

Finally, Reid Minich and Lynn Silvernale, with whom I shared the experiences described in the book, deserve special thanks for being patient with me during the weeks of my incessant questioning and checking to see if we all remembered the events as having happened in just that way.

In the land of
Joi Bangla

1

In the land of Joi Bangla

It's midnight. The windows are barred and shuttered. The doors are padlocked. Barbed wire is draped down the front stairs. A small black and white dog perches on a bamboo chair ready to yap at the slightest indication that thieves are on the prowl again. For this is Bangladesh — a hungry country!

Outside the sounds of humanity are still stirring. Cars speed by. A rickshaw driver jangles his bell. Babies cry. Old women pound the betel nut for the last chew of pan leaf before going to sleep. Men stroll by, and even at this hour someone is sure to shout "Joi Bangla!" ("Victory to Bengal!"). For this is Bangladesh — a happy country!

The hunger has always been here; the happiness is a new-comer.

I was a student nurse in Methodist Hospital School of Nursing in Brooklyn, New York, when I first witnessed the miracle of birth. I could not know then that one day, half a world away, I would be privileged to be an eyewitness to the birth of a nation.

Historians will probably agree that the emergence of Bangladesh as an independent nation was evident from the time of the partition of the subcontinent, into India and Pakistan, in 1947. But to those of us who lived through that time, it was a painful birth. As a nation, East Pakistan had little going for it. Separated from the rest of Pakistan by over 1100 miles of hostile territory, the east wing was always the outcast, the stepsister. The two wings had little in common. West Pakistanis

13

are tall, strong, military-oriented people; Bengalis are small-framed, lithe, and poetic by nature. West Pakistanis speak Urdu, a language similar in form and word to Arabic; Bengalis take pride in their Sanskrit-based Bengali tongue. West Pakistanis are wheat and bread-eating people; a Bengali feels he has not eaten unless rice is included in the menu. West Pakistanis excel in business; Bengalis are historically an agrarian people.

Even the climate defied unity. West Pakistan is a land of extremes: soaring mountains and barren deserts; mountain streams and hot, dry plains. Bengal is a country of rivers and lush fertile fields that sparkle like costly emeralds when the rice is growing in the low-lying paddies. Practically the only tie that bound the two parts of the country was the religion of Islam. And even that bond was weakened in the east wing by the percentage of Hindus who had intermingled with the Muslim majority.

With such flagrant differences underlying the very formation of the country of Pakistan, it is not difficult to see how and why discrimination began. Disparity was evident in many areas. Perhaps the most outstanding were these:

(1) Income from East Pakistan's resources and products — jute and tea, primarily — and the bulk of foreign aid received were disproportionately directed to West Pakistan to the neglect of the East. Earnings were used to finance imports for West Pakistan or as capital for industrial development.

(2) Economic policy favored the western half of the nation: tariffs, controls, and import licenses compelled the East to buy commodities from the West. Many times these were of inferior quality and actually could have been purchased at a cheaper rate from the regular world market.

(3) Opportunities for advancement and scholarships for study abroad were given in a far greater percentage to West Pakistan candidates.

The Planning Commission of the Government of Pakistan in its 1969-1970 report calculated that the per capita income of West Pakistan was 61 percent higher than the other half of the country.

But a man was to arise who would champion the cause of the downtrodden Bengalis. His name? Sheikh Mujibur Rahman — affectionately called "Mujib." He was no stranger to the Bengali people. Born into a middle-class family of landowners in 1919, he attended a mission school in a small town, then went on to the university in Calcutta and to law school in Dacca. It was there that he began organizing student demonstrations against the edict which would impose Urdu as the official language of the whole country. To accomplish this end, he founded the East Pakistan Students' League. For this activity he was thrown into jail, and throughout the next two decades he was in and out of various prisons. Just what his criminal activities were is all rather vague, but the West Pakistan military authorities considered him an enemy, a threat to Pakistan. Back in 1966 he produced his Six-Point Program which called for autonomy for East Pakistan: *autonomy,* not independence, not secession! Mujib's platform called for a virtual dismantling of the central government located in Islamabad, West Pakistan. The central government would have control of defense and diplomacy, while the two wings would hold jurisdiction over their own taxes, trade, and the use of foreign aid received.

Trouble hung in the air.

Life in Chittagong, even between cyclones and other natural disasters, was scarcely ever normal (whatever that is). But darker, more ominous clouds were threatening the shaky security of this land.

Political trouble was brewing.

In an attempt to pacify the restless East, whose population outnumbered the West by millions, a general election was promised for sometime in 1970.

The date for the election kept changing, partly because during those pre-election weeks the worst killer cyclone in the recorded history of man swept into the area taking an estimated 500,000 lives and rendering millions homeless.

With the initial shock of the devastation over, everyone's mind turned again to anticipation of the election. This was to be the first time in the country's twenty-two year history that a free and open election would be held.

But how do you campaign and conduct an election in a land where only 20 percent of the people are literate? How? You use pictures, of course. Every street corner, every lamppost, every free space on a wall bore the symbols of the various political parties. There were bicycles, oxcarts, elephants, measuring scales, umbrellas — objects in daily use with which the most illiterate could identify. Each of the more than twenty political parties had a symbol. But outweighing these lesser symbols by far was the mighty *noakha,* the sampan, emblem of Sheikh Mujibur Rahman's Awami League.

Day and night, loudspeakers blared out announcements of political rallies being held in the large fields, parks, and ball stadiums throughout the city. You had to keep track of which meeting was being held where, because driving through that part of town would be impossible. One evening I had to miss a meeting I started out to attend when I got caught in the midst of a rally — in the space of one hour I advanced only one city block. The city streets were littered with advertisements, slogans, and photos promising peace, prosperity and freedom from tyranny.

Finally the big day arrived — December 7, 1970. The masses thronged the streets to the schools, the community centers, and the courthouses where the volunteers sat to collect the completed ballots. For the first time, men and women, educated and uneducated, were given the opportunity to cast their vote. A day laborer rushed up to the office of his American supervisor. With tears in his eyes, he stuck out his thumb. "Look at that mark on my thumb," he cried. "That's where I gave my vote."

The election was fair and legal, but the outcome was unacceptable to the ruling military junta of West Pakistan.

Military President Yahya Khan had assumed that Sheikh Mujib and his Awami League might possibly win 60 percent of East Pakistan's allotment of 169 seats in the 313 seat National Assembly. The remaining East Pakistan delegates, Yahya figured, would align themselves with West Pakistani parties and prevent Mujib from winning a majority over the entire country. But in a stunning victory Mujib won 167 of the 169 seats — an overall majority in the assembly. The political and military powers of West Pakistan tried to pressure the Sheikh into compromising on his six-point mandate. Zulfiqar Ali Bhutto, leader of West Pakistan's People's Party which had won eighty seats, demanded that control of trade and foreign aid should remain within the jurisdiction of the central government. When the Sheikh refused to compromise on these points, Bhutto announced a boycott of the National Assembly scheduled to meet on 3 March 1971.

During the month of February meetings were held among all

the political leaders. These ended in deadlock. The Bengalis became incensed that the promises made before the election were not going to be allowed to be carried out. The hostilities of decades began to erupt in strikes and bloody riots between the Bengali majority and the non-Bengali, Bihari community. The *London Observer* in its 18 April 1971 edition defined the Biharis:

> These Urdu-speaking Muslims from the Indian state of Bihar came to East Pakistan as refugees in 1947 to escape Hindu persecution during the Partition troubles. The Biharis, mostly traders, soon took over the vacant shops left by Hindus who had run the other way. Now the Biharis have repaid Bengali hospitality by acting as scouts and guides for the West Pakistanis who are also Urdu-speaking and with whom they feel a greater solidarity.

When nighttime fell on the city of Chittagong, civilian jeeps delivered arms and ammunition, part of the army's stores, to non-Bengali homes. Suddenly those families had guests move in with them — commando units wearing civil dress. As these facts became known and the rumors rampaged, Bengalis began to distrust anyone who was not a Bengali.

The American missionaries were not excluded from the political turmoil. I had good reason to know.

It started out simply enough. One of the young people whose family attended our church services had contracted T.B. At the same time, the family was under heavy financial burdens and had the added care of knowing that the father in the family was dying with cancer. I took the entire family to be checked at the government T.B. clinic, then visited the authorities who run the sanitarium to see if we could get the boy into the hospital for free treatment. I drove him there, got him settled in, and promised I'd come back every week bringing some members of his family.

And then came Thursday, 18 February 1971.

The boy's mother, grandmother, ten-year-old sister, nineteen-year-old brother, and I went to visit him. We had a nice time together. I heard his complaints about the food and the service and generally concluded that he was getting on fine. On the way home, because the little sister had never seen the ocean, we veered off our route for a few minutes. There was a lot of construction equipment in the road: drums of tar, piles of rock and brick, and a parked car. Suddenly a little girl started across the road. I stepped on the brakes and honked the horn.

Instead of continuing across, the child turned around and laughingly called out, "Look! a *lady* is driving the car!"

Then she walked directly into my car.

I'll never be sure what happened next. Whether the brakes failed or whether the little girl rolled underneath — or what — I don't know. But in that instant, *I ran over her!*

My first instinct, of course, was to stop and see what I could do to help. Weaving in and out of the construction mess, trying to find a place to park, I heard nineteen-year-old Nirmal scream, "Go, sister, go *fast!*"

By that time hordes of people were upon us. Five-pound rocks and bricks were being hurled at us, and I lowered my head to the steering wheel to avoid the avalanche. Nirmal, thinking I had been killed, grabbed the wheel and frantically tried to turn us around. I sat back up and stepped on the accelerator, but the car had never had much power under the best circumstances and with the construction stuff all around I couldn't move far.

Mobs of people piled into the ever-present three-wheeled babi-taxis and bicycle rickshaws. They were soon forming a road-block ahead of me.

Then the trouble really began. They stole my car keys, tried to turn the car upside down, and hauled Nirmal out through the gaping hole where the windshield had been and began beating him.

The sequence of events is somewhat hazy, but suddenly a Pakistani engineer appeared. He sized up the situation, and sending an impressive-looking man over to the car, he himself went for the police. The person sent to guard us was a store-keeper who also was an elected member of the local government unit called the Union Council. He did a good job of holding the crowd at bay, all the while assuring us that if he had not come, we would all have been killed, but now that he was here, I should have no fear! In the midst of the ruckus Nirmal slipped away in a rickshaw for the six-mile trip to our mission's head-quarters in Chittagong, the Bible Information Center.

While Nirmal rode for help, the mother, grandmother, little sister, and I sat like an island in a sea of hostile faces.

"Foreigner!" "American!" "Christian!" were sneeringly hurled

at me again and again. I didn't dare shift my position at all,
for I was engulfed in splinters of glass and chunks of brick.

As the men insisted on pressing in on the car, the little girl
became hysterical. The mother tried to reason with the mob,
referring to me. "She is a medical person. Why don't you let
her help? Why will you not let us take the little girl to the
hospital? We have a good hospital. She would be okay there."

The old grandmother sat upright in her corner of the back
seat and never stopped mumbling, "O Jesus, O Jesus, O Jesus."

The accident occurred at 5:30 P.M. It was about 7:00 P.M.
when the Rev. Reid Minich, from our mission, arrived. (He had
taken off so fast when Nirmal gasped out the story that he
hadn't told the Rev. Gene Gurganus, veteran missionary nearing
completion of his third term in East Pakistan, where he was
going. Gene heard the word "accident" but nothing else.) To
us, sitting in that dark, cold, battered car not knowing what
was to become of us, Reid was a "knight in shining armor"
riding up on his Honda.

He took over and soon had us into a police car heading (he
thought) for home. The police driver had a different idea. He
took us to the police station where I was treated as "a criminal."
If I stood up, they told me to sit down. Eventually they let
Nirmal's family go, and they went straight to the Gurganus
home with the news of where we were.

In a little while Gene arrived. Now they had two prisoners!
Gene Gurganus, gracious Southern gentleman that he is, knew
that by this time I would be in need of a "comfort station."
Politely, he asked the officer in charge where the bathroom was.

"There isn't any," was the officer's crisp reply.

"Oh, come now," Gene said, "there must be a latrine or some
facility at this police station."

"You can't use it. You *cannot leave this room!*" The officer
was shouting now.

"You cannot deny a request such as this," Gene asserted.

The officer relented. Although it was dark outside, Gene
figured he'd better not push his luck by asking for a light; he
sent a boy across the road to a little shop to buy a candle.
Then we proceeded to the outhouse: one small boy carrying
a candle, one police guard, Gene Gurganus, and me.

At 9:30 P.M. Reid returned with all the legal entanglements
straightened out. "The Public," which consisted of the people

in the little girl victim's village (very little was ever heard of
her own parents), had not wanted the police brought into the
case at all. The Public established a price — 600 rupees (about
$125.00). It was a small settlement because (1) she was a
girl; (2) she had no education; (3) she was from a poor
family. The most tragic part to me was that not one of those
people expressed any concern whatever that a life had been lost.
The attitude was, "So what that she died! Everyone has to die."
The issue they wanted to make out of it was totally national-
istic and political: I was a foreigner. I had harmed a Bengali.

It was weeks later that we became aware of just how much
my being a non-Bengali had gone against us that day.

Nirmal was again visiting his brother at the T.B. hospital.
On an impulse, he stepped into a tea shop near the scene of
the accident and discreetly swung the conversation around to
that event.

"Do you remember an accident that happened near here
around the middle of February?" he asked.

"Oh, yes!" Everybody was eager to explain.

"There was a *white* lady driving the car," they all made quite
clear.

"What happened?" Nirmal led them on, and they filled in
their version of the details. Finally he asked, "Did the little
girl *die?*"

"Die! No, *she didn't die.* Do you want to see her?"

Nirmal was incensed. Telling us the story, he could scarcely
hold back his anger that we had been used to pad the pockets
of the local leaders, "The Public."

I didn't care one bit about that. The little girl had survived!
But I'll always have an indescribable feeling about the events
of that day.

The God who
watches over all

2

The God who watches over all

In those early months of 1971 our mission personnel were located in four areas scattered throughout the southern part of East Pakistan. Naturally, as tension mounted, the fate of each group was of concern to all the others. In the port city of Chittagong we were five adults and three children. Sixty-five miles to the south, at our Memorial Christian Hospital in Malumghat, lived nineteen adults and twenty-six children. Eight hours away by slow-moving country boat and torn-up road were one couple and their two small boys at Hebron, our jungle station, on the edge of the Chittagong Hill tracts. And off in a different direction in the remote town of Barisal, where the Oriental Institute (a language school for missionaries) is located, we had eight adults and seven children. Our greatest concern was for this group because our brand-new recruits were among them. Later, as they shared their story with us, we were reminded that God is able to take infinitely better care of His volunteers than the most experienced senior missionary ever could!

"Our first hint of trouble," Dr. Joe DeCook, a first-term missionary from Northern Michigan, told us, "was when, in February, the postal strike was called. Not only were those of us in Barisal cut off from the outside world, but now there was no way for us to get in touch with the rest of our mission family.

"We noticed the heightening of tension among our language

teachers, especially the Hindus. During the last weeks in February they were almost unable to teach because of worry and agitation.

"Since a nationwide postal strike had been successful, we felt that a transportation strike would be the next step. This would leave us stranded in Barisal. With our Mission Field Council meetings scheduled for March 8, we booked reservations on a steamer going to Chittagong on March 5.

"On March 1, however, Yahya Khan ordered the postponement of the National Assembly, and an outburst of violence broke over the entire country. The ruling powers clamped restrictions on town and city. Bengalis protested by refusing to work or continue normal services.

"That finished school for that term! On the morning of March 5, aware that our ship would not be sailing, we started to look for other ways to get out of Barisal. A road that would take us north to the capital city of Dacca involved a ferryboat across a wide river, and with communications completely disrupted, we had no guarantee the ferry would be operating. Normally, a train runs to Chittagong, but here again, would it be running? And in any case, in order to get to the railhead we would have to travel by steamer or boat. Even had these means been available to us, it did not seem wise to take such an entourage — our party of fifteen and all the baggage — out on public highways with the country being such a live volcano. We could find no private transportation — not even a rowboat that would take us directly to Chittagong.

"There was an occasional ship still running for the purpose of evacuating people out through Dacca, but we had no way of getting from Dacca to Chittagong. Taking the evacuation ship would have meant we were leaving East Pakistan, and none of us wanted to do that. Some of us didn't have valid visas to get us back in should we leave. On March 5, with just a half-hour notice, the other language students left. (We hadn't known that the ship was leaving; we learned the next day.)"

Dr. and Mrs. DeCook had a feeling that the time had come to pack their goods into fifty-five gallon drums and seal them as if they were to be shipped to the end of the earth. That "feeling" proved providential. The Beals, second-termers taking a refresher language course, were veterans of Pakistan crises. How could they know this would be any different from those they had already weathered? But Marjorie Beals, acting on an inner urge, stole some hours from her study time and completed a project she had always meant to get done. She sorted and pasted the precious photographs of children, friends, and events into albums and placed these on the bottom of the suitcase she was taking for the one-week stay at the Field Council meetings!

Her husband, Mel Beals, and Bob Adolph, our lab technologist, were glued to the dock on Sunday, March 7, not knowing whether or not a ship was coming. Suddenly they heard a faint whistle in the distance. Pedaling their bikes as fast as they could, they rushed to the apartments and alerted everyone to leave — NOW! They packed people and baggage into the VW minibus and in just forty-five minutes they were on the dock. Joe De-Cook raced back to the house, locked the car in the garage, jumped in a rickshaw, and told the driver he would pay him extra if he made the two miles to the pier in time.

Dr. DeCook continues the story from here.

"Monday evening found us safe in Chittagong. Gene Gurganus had been meeting steamers from Barisal all week — those scheduled that never arrived; so when our unscheduled one did arrive, we had to go and get him. On the drive in from the port to the city we learned that on March 6, the day we were scheduled to arrive, there had been terrible fighting out on the docks. Had God delayed our ship to protect us from that?

"God did something else special for us — the over and abundantly that we read about and that the friends back home petition for us in prayer. We were safe down at Malumghat, our hospital station. But up there in Barisal, in those three vacated apartments, were thousands of dollars' worth of equipment: cameras, tape recorders, radios, appliances, household goods, and clothes. Until the military took complete control late in May, Barisal was a haven for hoodlums. Lawlessness and disorder were the rule. The house next to ours was completely stripped by sixteen robbers working in broad daylight. It was known that three American families had lived in a certain house — and that we had left! The night watchmen hired by the landlord to sleep in the stairwell would have run away if an owl had hooted too loudly.

"Mel Beals and I returned to Barisal in June to survey the damage. The house had been broken into once; a camera and some clothes had been taken, but the bulk of the things were there. We packed up beds, stoves, refrigerators, and drums of household goods and got the mountain of stuff to the docks. Ships were coming into Barisal once every ten days, and we were told they were carrying only military goods.

"The shipping master looked at the stuff, and exclaimed, 'This is impossible.' Then, turning around slowly, he said, 'You guys are in a mess. I'm going to do whatever is necessary to get this down to Chittagong for you.' And he did! Everything arrived safely in Chittagong. In those days that was nothing short of a miracle.

"God didn't have to do that for us. But it was His equipment, and He saw fit to keep it safe."

In yet one other way God showed His special care for our group. Our high school young people were all home for winter vacation from Murree Christian School in West Pakistan. The new semester was about to begin; for four of them it was the final semester before graduation. Naturally the parents were hesitant about sending the four girls and three boys away with the impending trouble in the country, and yet if it materialized here, it might be better to have these teenagers settled in school. Those who live at the hospital came up to Chittagong on March 9 intending to go by train to Dacca, then out to West Pakistan. The plan was that they would travel with the other East Pakistan missionary kids attending Murree. In fact, our teenagers always became the guardians for the little ones going away to boarding school. Very early on March 10 they went to the train station, only to be told that there were no tickets available. That left only one way open: an all-day trip in the VW bus from Chittagong to Dacca.

Rev. Jay Walsh, who accompanied the young people, relates their frustrations in attempting to get a flight to West Pakistan.

"On March 11 we learned that because of the great scramble for seats aboard planes bound for West Pakistan, the government had closed the ticket counters and instituted a new system.

People lined up were given a number. Number 1 had been issued on March 6. On the eleventh of March our high school students were given numbers 3319 - 3325!

"We had to make frequent trips to the airport to find how the numbers were moving along. There were two or three flights a day, and we never knew when our numbers would be called. Flying time to West Pakistan had more than doubled due to India's having forbidden the Pakistan International Airlines to fly over her territory. This meant that flights had to circumnavigate India and touch down in Colombo, Ceylon.

"The airport was filled with people who were fleeing the country. I watched a man drag a small box over to the weigh-in counter — a box of *solid gold*. (People's wealth was more often in cash or gold ornaments rather than money in the bank.) The merchants and business people who were running to West Pakistan for shelter were taking the wealth of the country with them."

The flights arriving from Karachi were just as crowded as those departing for the West, only the passengers aboard were not settlers going to a new land. Those planes were loaded with West Pakistan troops, armed and ready for combat.

The numbers crept up, and finally on March 14 our young people boarded the last day's flight to Karachi. From there they went to the Murree Hills and back to school.

No one could know that it would be a long time before these missionary kids would hear from or about their parents and friends back home in East Pakistan.

God decided for us

3

God decided for us

President Yahya Khan's announcement of the indefinite post-ponement of the National Assembly sparked the tinderbox on which we had been sitting. Clashes, riots, and arson spread throughout the city.

One night one of the preachers in our church came asking for clothing, quilts, or sleeping mats for a church family. He told us that the whole top of a hill had been burned off when some men attempted to make bombs and Molotov cocktails.

The Pakistan military decided to step in, using force to control the "miscreants" (a word they interpreted as meaning any-one who did not absolutely kowtow to the rules of military law). In the controlling of the disturbance, the military con-ceded that 172 persons had been killed. The Dacca corres-pondent for the *London Observer* set the figure at nearer 2000 people killed in Dacca alone.

Despite this provocation, the Awami League refrained from declaring independence. Rather, on March 7, in a speech to the nation, Sheikh Mujibur Rahman launched the noncoopera-tion, nonviolence movement. He asked the people to refrain from paying taxes and tariffs into the central government's coffers and that no one aid the military in any way. He also ordered the violence and killings to cease. In an attempt to halt the bitter communal riots among the various nationalities, he de-clared, "Anyone living in Bengal is a Bengali."

The terrible incidents did stop. And though, in protest against the existing regime, policemen refused to go to their posts, traffic did flow smoothly and law and order seemed to prevail.

Yahya Khan set March 25 for the convening of the National Assembly. The Sheikh replied that in order for him to attend, the following conditions had to be met:

1. Martial law had to be lifted.
2. The soldiers had to return to their barracks.
3. A commission of inquiry had to be set up to look into the military killing of Bengalis in the major cities.
4. The government had to be turned over to the newly elected officers.

The campaign of noncooperation effectively transferred civilian authority to Sheikh Mujib, but still he remained committed to the unity of Pakistan, as demonstrated by the fact that he continued to take part in the talks and negotiations despite the well-advertised influx of West Pakistani troops. A review of the whole situation would seem to indicate that those peace talks were never in good faith; rather, they were delaying tactics until the military could bring in sufficient troops and supplies to unleash a reign of terror.

During our annual Field Council meetings that second week of March, we spent much time in the discussion of contingency plans.

Ours is a mission that believes in and practices teamwork. We try to work through a situation or problem until we mutually reach a decision. But this was something different. We all felt that the decision to stay or leave must be that of the individual or the family; no one would be coerced into staying, nor would anyone be made to feel like a quitter if he decided to get out.

The large missionary group at Malumghat Hospital considered the possibility of emergency exit by boats to a waiting ocean-going rescue vessel or, as an alternative, leaving through the neighboring country of Burma (see map).

Those of us living in Chittagong had been among the foreign community who received a letter stating that if we wished to leave the country we should proceed to a particular hilltop compound to await the arrival of RAF planes.

Sunday night, March 21, the Chittagong staff met to discuss our plans. The Gurganus family were due for furlough within a few weeks. They reasoned that this plane might be a good way for them to proceed home. With Gene Gurganus gone,

Reid Minich would be the only male missionary left—he couldn't leave. Lynn Silvernale, with whom I shared an apartment in the heart of the city, and I felt no leading to pack up and pull out. We three voted to stay.

March 23—Pakistan Day! Officially this is a day set aside to celebrate the founding and continuation of Pakistan, but this time it was also commemorating a day of mourning for those who suffered in the Bengali struggle for freedom. The green, red, and gold flag of Bangladesh flew on every house, store, and car. Only on the Dacca radio station and the Government House was Pakistan's star and crescent seen.

As if to further drive home the point that Pakistan would stay cemented together, that very day a Pakistani ship, the *M V SWAT* landed in Chittagong harbor carrying its deadly load of arms and ammunition. News of the ship's arrival spread rapidly, and the city burst into anger. Uprooted trees, empty tar drums, slabs of cement, disabled vehicles—everything available was strewn on the roadways to prevent troops and supplies from getting to the army cantonment area. Thousands of Bengalis armed with sticks and lead pipes stormed to the port area to oppose the unloading of the ship. It was a pitiful sight—such courage, but such total lack of preparation or organization!

Dock workers, following Sheikh Mujib's orders, refused to unload the ship, so recruits from the Bengali regiment were pressed into service. "The ammunition must be unloaded at all costs," the West Pakistani brigadier was heard to say. And the cost was paid—in the blood of Bengalis. How many died, how many were injured on the docks, no one will ever know.

The captain of the ship was himself a Bengali. What thoughts must have haunted him as he realized the destruction that he was bringing to his own people! Upon arrival in port, he locked himself in the bathroom of his cabin. Three days later, throwing himself upon the mercy of the mobs on the dock, he called, "Come and kill me if you will." Friends rescued him and hid him in safety until the war was over.

On March 26 we awoke to hear the Chittagong radio station, in speaking about the Sheikh's noncooperation movement, hail this day as the "twenty-fifth glorious day of the struggle." What we did not know, and did not learn until many weeks later, was that the "glorious struggle" was over in Dacca—at least

temporarily. *Time* magazine's April 5 edition described the
night of March 25.

> In Dacca, army tanks and truckloads of troops with fixed
> bayonets came clattering out of their surburban base, shouting
> "Victory to Allah" and "Victory to Pakistan." Before long,
> however, howitzer tank artillery and rocket blasts rocked half
> a dozen scattered sections of Dacca. The chatter of automatic
> weapons was punctuated with grenade explosions, and tall
> columns of black smoke towered over the city.

The next week's edition of *Time,* April 12, elaborated.

> Tanks rolled through Dacca, blowing houses to bits. At the
> university, soldiers slaughtered students inside the buildings.
> Near Dacca's marketplace, Urdu-speaking government soldiers
> ordered Bengali-speaking townspeople to surrender, then
> gunned them down when they failed to comply. Bodies lay in
> mass graves at the university, in the old city, and near the
> municipal dump.

But we in Chittagong knew nothing of this. At 8:45 A.M.
the Dacca radio station abruptly played the national anthem and
went off the air. Chittagong's station aired only taped music.

Our friends, Mr. and Mrs. Thomas Dass, had come to visit us.
Mrs. Dass, a former school teacher, is Lynn Silvernale's national
co-worker. Lynn, a nurse who learned the essentials of linguis-
tics, has for the past four years been engaged in Bible translation. She works from the original Greek, preparing a simplified
English version of various books of the New Testament. Mrs.
Dass is her Bengali counterpart. Using Lynn's English base, she
writes the first draft of the Bengali common language New Testament.

But Mrs. Dass had not come to work. She and her godly
husband had come to warn us of possible danger. We talked
and prayed and sang together. Mr. Dass taught us a new song,
a hauntingly beautiful Indian melody to the words:

> O Jesus, You are mine;
> Save my life, my Jesus.
>
> Those who are sinful may come to Him;
> Lord, give me salvation.
>
> The river is deep; the boat is small;
> Lord, carry me across.
>
> In You I am victorious;
> Come, Lord, give me strength.

We were all going to need God's strength as the rivers proved to be deep, and the boat small.

While our friends were still with us, we turned the radio on to hear the regular 10:00 A.M. news. Instead, we tuned into the *fifteen new edicts of the martial law regime*. Among them:

> No group of more than five people allowed to gather together.
>
> No political meetings to be held.
>
> All guns to be turned in to military headquarters.
>
> All duplicating machines, or any machine capable of reproducing printed material, to be turned in to military headquarters.
>
> Everyone to return to work immediately.
>
> Etc., etc., etc.

Even as those orders were being translated into English, we heard the clamoring of protesting Bengalis out on the streets. The Dasses left quickly, anxious to get back to the rest of their household safely. Watching them go, we looked across to the parking lot where men crowded into old World War II trucks. The cries of "Joi Bangla" were tumultuous as the truckloads of stick-waving patriots pulled away. Those shouts were nine months premature.

Reid walked over from his house around the corner. "Have you heard the latest rules?" he asked. "This doesn't sound good."

"I'd feel a lot safer if you could stay here," I admitted.

"Well, I'll stay for awhile, but I can't stay indefinitely," he replied.

Just before 8:00 P.M. that Friday evening, we turned on the radio to locate the station which would carry President Yahya Kahn's speech to the nation. Suddenly we heard a loud voice carrying clearly through the streets. I thought it was a loudspeaker blaring more orders. Looking out from the verandah, we saw groups of people clustered in front of any doorway where there was a radio. We turned the dial on our own radio until the voices blended into one. Then we listened, mesmerized, to the voice of Sheikh Mujibur Rahman announcing that he had declared East Pakistan to be independent—*free Bangladesh*.

He called to his people: "Come out of your houses with whatever weapons you have. Resist the enemy forces at any cost . . . until the last enemy soldier is vanquished from our sacred soil."

What we did not know was that this was a prerecorded tape. For the night before, after unsuccessful talks, Yahya Kahn had flown out of Dacca at midnight. Much later, we heard the rumor that in the luggage compartment of his plane had crouched a political prisoner — *Sheikh Mujibur Rahman.*

Right on schedule, Yahya Khan started his speech. With few preliminaries, he began his tirade against the Sheikh.

"The man and his party are enemies of Pakistan. This crime will not go unpunished. We will not allow some power-hungry and unpatriotic people to destroy this country and play with the destiny of 120,000,000 people."

Pakistan's president called the Sheikh a traitor. He stated that he himself had tried to come to a peaceful settlement, but that he had been unable to reason with Mujib. Then he banned the entire Awami League. (That would be comparable to banning the Republican party after President Nixon had won the election.)

I was getting ready for bed at 11:00 P.M when the Voice of America reported, "Sheikh Mujibur Rahman has declared East Pakistan a sovereign, independent state to be called Bangladesh."

At 11:30, as I was shutting out my light, the shots began. At first it was a pop-pop-pop. I looked to see if people were celebrating the Sheikh's declaration by shooting off firecrackers. The streets were empty. While I was staring out my window, the shots increased in volume and intensity. I ran to Lynn's room and found her waking from a foggy sleep. Cautiously we moved from window to window. If this was fireworks and people were rejoicing, where were the people? Between each blast, everything outside was black and deathly still. We stood at our screened-in dining area looking towards the city center. As we watched, four huge balls of fire shot across the sky between the two houses behind us. Finally we realized it wasn't fireworks.

We moved our mattresses into the living room, the most central place in the house, and tried to sleep. The shots continued till dawn. Interspersed with the pop-pop sounds were the ra-ta-tats of machine guns.

Things seemed quiet and normal again on Saturday morning, so we dug into the yearly task of canning vegetables for the six

lean months when little is available. We washed and chopped
and bottled carrots, potatoes, okra, onions, beans, and tomatoes.
Only when we had twelve quart jars ready and a full pan waiting
its turn did we discover that the pressure cooker didn't work.
All the vegetables would have to be eaten within a few days
or our money, time, and energy would be wasted.

Reid arrived mid-morning with the news that he had just given
his car away. This was no small matter; it was our only means
of escape, but he had felt that he had to do it. He could never
again preach the love of God if he, God's messenger, failed to
display that love. The man who came requesting the car was
Menindro Das, a convert from Hinduism. Back in 1966, Menindro and his wife and mother, one by one, had placed their faith
in Christ. Since that time, Menindro's in-laws had publicly
disgraced and disowned them. Although they lived close together, they never visited each other; the relatives refused to
contaminate themselves by contact with Christians. Now, however, prophetically sizing up what the lot of Hindus would be
in the purge about to begin, his father-in-law begged Menindro
to take the whole family to some safe "Christian place." How
could Reid refuse to provide the vehicle for escape?

"Do you want to get down to the hospital too?" Reid asked
us. "I think I could still catch the driver before he leaves."

Again we chose to stay.

Reid was scarcely out the door when Gene Gurganus came
over on his cycle to check on us. He told of driving past the
Pakistan Naval Headquarters where guns were aimed at pedes-
trians out in the road. In the next breath he announced that
he had come to take us, riding on the back of his motorcycle
and Reid's motorcycle, over to his house. An American community had been set up for all the foreigners in the city. Flying
high on the roof were the Canadian and American flags.

What should we do? Was our first responsibility to be in a
place where we were with our other missionaries and fellow
Americans so that the missionary men would not have the responsibility of us on their heads, or was our first responsibility
to the nationals whom we had come to serve? While we were
weighing this, the oldest brother in the Boshu family came plead-
ing for a safe place for his mother and the younger children.

The Lord made the decision for us. We couldn't turn them
out. We couldn't take them with us to the American set-up. So

we stayed. Reid had already told us that he would stick with us if we felt that we needed him—we did.

Who were the Boshus? Sara Boshu, eighteen-years-old, was to be married on Good Friday, just three weeks away. Her fiance lived and worked in the part of town where the Bengali-Bihari riots were most violent. We completely lost track of him and assumed that he had been killed. Ten months later, a weary, worn young man, he was to return from months of wandering, and living with relatives and refugees across the border in India.

Rebecca was a giggly teenager. To her war was another adventure to add to her list. The foresighted Christian boarding school she attended wisely decided to return their students to their homes just before the war broke out. Had they not, she would have been stranded over one hundred miles from Chittagong—a day and a half journey by train and steamer.

Lucky and Beauty were two frightened little girls who couldn't quite understand what this was all about, and Shapon was a little boy with dancing eyes and eagerness to try anything.

Shapon had always been a great favorite of ours. A few years back he had helped us Americans broaden our concept of the Christ who transcends all language barriers. It happened like this.

A new missionary, Monte (Marilyn) Malmstrom, had arrived. The Bengali-speaking children in Sunday school, though quite unable to communicate with her in words, recognized a kindred spirit. Here was someone who liked children, sincerely, for their own sakes.

Lynn had taught the children to participate in prayer, and they frequently decided just who was to pray on a given occasion.

It was not surprising, then, that during the class came the eager request, "We want Miss Monte to pray." The entire class took up the chant in Bengali, "We want Miss Monte."

"But," Lynn protested, "Monte can't speak Bengali; she would have to pray in English."

Shapon's dark eyes filled with questioning wonder, and he asked, "Doesn't Jesus understand English?"

The mother of the Boshu family was a hard-working, godly woman striving under dreadful odds to follow the Lord.

And there was old "Didi-Ma," Grandma. She was deafer than the deafest post. Every time someone would cringe and run to the shelter away from the firing, she'd say, "I don't know what you are all so excited about. This is nothing like the Second World War." Of course she could hear *then*.

There were people missing from the Boshu family. The *oldest brother*—a careworn young man bearing far too heavy burdens in trying to keep this family together. The *middle brother*—convalescing in the government T.B. hospital. This institution was exactly at the point on the edge of the city where the Pakistani military and the freedom fighters clashed. The doctors and hospital staff fled for their lives, leaving a hospital full of patients in varying stages of tuberculosis. They stayed on for a few days, hiding under the beds as the fire passed on all sides. When the food ran out, those who could walk started a four-day trek through the hills and wooded outskirts surrounding the city, trying to find any place of shelter. But what happened to those who were too sick to walk?

The *youngest brother, Nirmal* — eager to be of help to those of us in the house, but not wanting to stay still long enough to find out what he could do to help. Every time he went out on his forays for food or other supplies, his mother lived in fear and trembling that we'd never see him again.

One other was missing. On March 2, the morning of the first city-wide general strike, closing down all traffic, Lynn and I had heard a knock on our door.

"Could you come quickly, please? My father is very sick."

Going out into the cold predawn air, we walked the quarter mile between our house and the Boshus' two-room bamboo house. We had made the trip often in the past few weeks since Mr. Boshu was returned from our hospital. They had operated hoping to find a perforated ulcer which could be removed. Instead, his abdomen had been full of cancerous growth. We had been able to give him rest and some degree of comfort through various injections. We had provided nourishing food to stimulate his appetite. But now he was gone. We huddled in the six-by-nine foot room, each of us hugging one of the little girls and offering what consolation we could to the family shivering with sorrow, fear, and cold. Then the realization of the immediate problems hit us. On this strike day, nothing would be allowed to move. How could we bury their father? How could the service be conducted? How could word be passed on to family and friends? The boys were afraid to walk around too

much in the early hours in case they would be picked up for
suspicious activity, so Lynn, Reid and I began to walk.

The funeral could be held in the Church of England diagon-
ally across the main street from the Boshu house. Word of the
death got passed around, and people walked, some of them two
miles or more, to pay their respects. But how would we get
the body to the cemetery three miles out of the city? There was
no solution but to take the chances involved and get out a car.
In this land with no embalming facilities and with the heat of the
day increasing in intensity, there was no possibility of postponing the burial until the strike was over. Reid Minich backed his
Landrover (that always needed a push to get started) out onto
the main road and prayed it across to the church. Following the
ceremony, there was a long haggle as to who would go to the
cemetery. Finally the procession pulled out, two student friends
of the boys sitting on the hood of the car and as many as could
fit crowded around the back, all shouting "dead body, dead
body" as they made their way to the burial ground.

Now twenty-four days after the funeral, the Boshu family
came to our house to stay. Minutes after they arrived, Jabbor,
the young man who has worked for us for many years, arrived
with his wife. She was wearing the black burka over her face
and carrying one baby and leading a two-year-old. They had
carried what they could and left the rest behind—to be stolen.
Our "refugee camp" was filling up.

For these and others who would join our household, tense,
fearful days lay ahead.

The diary entry for March 28 reads: "It sure doesn't seem
like Sunday. We cooked and cooked a flat pancake-like bread
called puri for breakfast. Afterwards, Reid went to his house
to shower and shave. There is very little water here. The
Bengalis turned off the water mains for our area so that the
military holed up in the naval headquarters will suffer. We're
nearly out of kerosene too. Thank God the power has stayed
on so we can cook with the electric appliances."

Throughout the day, Radio Free Bangladesh came on the air
again and again making the same announcement.

"Mankind! It is reported that more troops have come by sea
and air from West Pakistan. Therefore I request all democratic
nations to come to the aid of the freedom-loving people of
Bangladesh."

Then, speaking in Bengali, the announcer called for all the citizens of Chittagong to go to a general meeting area, carrying their concealed weapons with them. They were to be organized into fighting units. People in our neighborhood did respond. We watched the men leave their homes. But how can you conceal a hunting rifle or a hoe? As it became obvious that people carrying guns were being shot on sight, the order to meet at the central place was rescinded. Instead, people were told to stay in their own neighborhoods. Captains from the Bengali Liberation Army would come and organize them into fighting squads.

Radio stations from the "outside world" carried the news that twenty-five foreign correspondents had been expelled from Dacca. Loren Jenkins, reporting in *Newsweek,* April 12, explained.

> We had seen too much to suit the Pakistani army . . . . We were told to pack and be ready to go in a half hour . . . . Two hours later, we were herded into four army trucks and taken under guard to Dacca's airport, where we were searched and most of our notes and films confiscated. A Pakistani civilian jetliner flew us to Karachi in West Pakistan where we were searched again. My typewriter and radio were dismantled, and two rolls of film I had hidden in the radio's battery compartment were seized. I was then taken into another room and stripped, and a packet of film that I was carrying in my underwear was taken. "You will have only your memory left," a police official chortled cheerfully.

At 4:30 P.M. we held our Sunday worship service. Reid spoke from Psalm 91. Besides giving us strength and encouragement, he had found a pun in the Bengali Bible. The "pestilence that walketh in darkness" (vs. 6) is translated by the word "Bihari" in Bengali—and we weren't to be afraid of it!

Reid called for various ones to lead in prayer. Young Shapon started first. After the usual flowery phrases which nearly every Bengali feels are necessary in approaching God, Shapon got to the point.

"Lord, You know we have no more water, and it is very inconvenient living without water. Please send us some."

Our God who hears the prayers of little boys praying in Bengali was about to answer Shapon's plea.

In the presence
of my enemies

4

In the presence
of my enemies

During the closing minutes of our service that Sunday afternoon we heard heavy firing—very near us. Shooting and killing were occurring at the crossroad to the left of our narrow little street. Soon we heard the heavy tread of boots on our stairs. The remnants of the Bengal Regiment and the newly formed Liberation Army were bringing us their wounded.

"Of course we will help you," we told them. "But we have one big problem. We have no water."

Without a second's delay the leader dispatched boys to the nearest well. An organized bucket brigade went into action.

Shapon was delighted at the answer to his prayer, as he watched buckets full of water being carried into our house.

We knelt on the floor to tend the wounded.

The first man had been shot in the leg as the jeep he was riding in rounded the corner beneath the hill where the government official, the District Commissioner, had lived.

This wounded man's buddies thought that the bullet was still in his leg. One of them wanted to dig around with a rusty penknife. In case we couldn't persuade the friend otherwise, Lynn decided to medicate the patient so he could feel no pain. She gave him 100 mg. of Demerol—quite a normal dose for an adult in the States, but a real whopper for the smaller-framed, undernourished Bengalis. In the end, the friend backed out and left me to dig around in the wounded leg with a hemostat clamp. I had never been exposed to gunshot wounds and had no idea what I was digging for. Reid explained what it would be like if the bullet had entered the leg whole, and that if it had shattered first, it would feel like pea-sized pellets.

I don't know where that bullet went, but we never found it in the man's leg. By the time we had finished probing, he was sound asleep. Apart from a few minutes when Mrs. Boshu forced him to eat and drink a little, he was "out" for the night.

The next man was badly injured. He had five deep bullet wounds in his legs and serious skull injuries. He needed surgery —much more than Lynn and I could do for him. After applying first aid, we let him go, with the soldiers promising that they would get him to Medical College Hospital. Whether they were able to or not, we never knew.

Others had cuts to be washed and bandaged. All the time we were treating one of the men, he sat fingering a Chinese-made hand grenade. His friend relieved him of his rifle and while taking it out on the landing, accidentally fired it. The wounded man was furious at this mistake because ammunition was so scarce that every shot had to count.

"I'd rather give my *life* than a bullet," he declared.

While I was in the midst of this probing for bullets and shrapnel, a neighbor from the next lane came over to ask if I had any tranquilizers.

"My wife cannot sleep," he explained.

My first reaction was anger that he was taking up our time with such a silly thing. Couldn't sleep—so who *could* sleep? What a petty problem when people were bleeding and dying on the street in front of us. Then I remembered that that lady didn't have resources upon which to rely. She couldn't, as I had done each night while lying there trying to sleep with the roars and rumblings of mortar shells and machine gun fire all around, begin to recite the verses perhaps even unconsciously memorized; "I will both lay me down and rest in peace, for thou Lord, only maketh me to dwell in safety," and "He giveth His beloved sleep."

The patients left. We tried to clean up the mess, but didn't want to waste our precious supply of water.

Our next visitors were Menindro and the driver safely back from Malumghat and points south where they had left their families. We were doubly glad and thankful for their safety, for now Reid's car was back and available should we need it. On the return trip the car had been stopped and searched repeatedly; the engine had been examined and the front seat and toolbox pulled out.

Menindro brought us news and notes from our colleagues down at the hospital. We laughed when reading them. The group there was so far removed from us, crouching on the floor in our blacked-out room. They had no way of knowing what was going on a mere sixty-five miles from them. They asked us to consider going down there, and when we came would we please bring them "money from the bank, food from the store, sewing from the tailor."

The banks were closed; the food shops were looted; the tailor had probably been killed!

It was dark by then and too dangerous to go out, so Menindro, the driver, his friend, and our "knocked-out" patient took over the living room. They played the radio softly. The last words we heard from Radio Free Bangladesh that night were, "In the name of 'discipline,' they're digging a graveyard."

On Monday morning, eighteen of us sat around the living room eating a breakfast of puffed rice and tea. The man with the bullet in his leg decided he needed to return to duty. Nirmal walked with him to the end of our street. As they rounded the corner, the soldier joined a man who was carrying a gun. Immediately there was a shot from the top of the hill, and one man fell. Nirmal dashed back to the house to tell us that our patient had been killed.

We had hardly had time to feel sorry when he appeared at the door unscathed, saying, "I lost my bandage. Will you fix me another one?"

With shooting intensifying on all sides, we set up Lynn's room as a dispensary. Then we discovered how poorly equipped we were to be a field hospital. We didn't even have a rolled bandage! I groaned as I thought about all the ladies' missionary groups who had offered to send them. I had always refused, saying that our hospital still had drums full. Now when we needed bandages we had to set the kids to ripping and rolling our sheets.

Going from room to room, we pushed all of the furniture in front of the windows. This made it dark throughout the house, but provided extra footage for the bullets to lodge in before they got to us. That morning we also made some policy decisions regarding the food and kerosene problems. The three Americans would eat only tinned food from our closely hoarded stock. The Bengalis then would be able to eat what fresh food was available. Along with the rice which Jabbor and Nirmal managed to bring from the bazaar, they fried the carrots, potatoes, okra, onions, beans, and tomatoes which we had cut and not been able to can the Saturday before. While we had felt so frustrated and wondered how we could keep from wasting all those vegetables, God knew all about the needs we would have. I found myself thinking, "Isn't God clever?"

We decided we would save the little bit of kerosene we had in case the electricity went off and we must use the kerosene stove. That meant when the refrigerator ran out of kerosene, we would have to turn it off permanently—and that could happen any minute. The needle had been registering empty for two days. We also rationed out drinking water, baths, and radio listening.

Radio Free Bangladesh had no set schedule. It was just there or not there. It was exciting to hear the announcer begin with a "Joi Bangla" in the midst of the firing outside. Sara, Rebecca, and I did a little dance around the living room each time the station came back on. It was a boost to know that they were still there. In order not to miss them, I left the radio on whether there was any broadcast or not. The attachment which allowed the radio to run off electricity got too hot and burned out, and we were reduced to using batteries which were not "ever-ready."

Tuning in to the Radio Pakistan station, we heard them complain bitterly that India, the British Broadcasting Company, and Voice of America had no right to refer to Bangladesh. Pakistan insisted that the trouble was over. The military was in full control; everything was back to normal. The shops were open, and people were out on the streets. Air India, on the other hand, quoted Mrs. Indira Gandhi as saying that this was "the genocide of the Bengali people!"

People were concerned for our welfare. Many of them risked danger to come out to see if we were safe. Men from our church, some of our young people, and the Dasses came when they could. Some of them had seen truckloads of bodies being driven out of the city. Some had read notices advising families, especially women and children, to get out of the city. Despite the morale-building speeches, including more prerecorded tapes of the Sheikh saying, "I am alive and

well in Chittagong," Bengalis were discouraged. Their East
Bengal Regiment, a crack troop during World War II days,
had been in key positions up on the hilltops, but they had
no arms or ammunition to back them up, and the positions
couldn't be held.

Rachel, the Dasses' thirteen-year-old daughter, was frightened. Her parents made us promise that if we went away,
we would take her with us.

That Monday afternoon two young fellows from our church,
Stephen and Paul (whom we've always called by his nick-
name, "Babla"), ducked into our house between rounds of
heavy firing. Pakistani planes were flying overhead, and flames
burst into the sky in many directions. The boys waited for a
lull and then dashed back to their homes. We told them not
to try coming again.

We met again at 4:30 to read the Bible and pray together.
As we finished, a whole family appeared at the door. They
were from one of the areas where we had watched houses disap-
pear in flames. This family had been inside, listening to the
radio, when a stray bullet came through the window. In trying
to dodge the spray, the young wife had fallen and broken her
wrist. We gave her pain medication, and wrapping cloth around
a bamboo pole split lengthwise, we splinted and bandaged her
arm.

That night after the food had been cooked and supper eaten,
the electricity went off. We all sat on the floor in the living
room, keeping very quiet so that we could have the door open
and get a little breeze. To help pass the time, we softly quoted
Bible verses from memory. Trying to say them in Bengali soon
depleted *our* stock, and the children ran out fast too. Next we
tried the game, "Do what I *say in English.*" We would say the
English phrase slowly and the little children would act out
what we said. We were doing "Open the door," "Shut the door,"
when old Didi-Ma came in.

"What do you want to shut the door for? It's too hot in
here," she complained, not knowing what we were doing.

We convulsed in giggles then and really had to shut the door
so the sound of our voices couldn't be heard by any trigger-
happy snipers out on the street.

We all went to our assigned sleeping rooms, but none of us
could sleep. Our plan was that when the shelling came too

close to the house, we would leave the rooms we were in and, half crawling, work our way past the open area to the living room which had been turned into a bomb shelter. The furniture was lined up around the walls, and cushions and rugs covered the windows. The room became a cozy cocoon, although a cocoon with fourteen people in it is not the most comfortable place. Chitra, the dog, was out on the verandah, but the whine of the shells hurt her ears and she howled every time a new barrage began. We finally opened the door to let her in with us.

Sara was lying in the middle of the floor with her arms straight up in the air. She waved them methodically, trying to shoo off the mosquitoes. Chitra took a good look at her, then lay down beside her, rolled on her back, and stuck all four paws up in the air. We watched these antics by the light of one tiny candle and laughed hysterically at the pair. That laughter calmed everybody, and we settled down to sleep or to private battles with the mosquitoes.

Toward morning the power came back on, and we slept undisturbed as the big whirling overhead fan whooshed the mosquitoes away. But lest we get too many minutes of unbroken sleep, the shooting started again: loud, heavy ammunition and mortar attacks.

The lady with the broken arm returned that morning. Obviously she had missed the whole point of her treatment for she had carefully undone the splint and bandage when she took her bath. We started again, this time with three sticks and firm strips of adhesive tape. We advised her husband to take her to the Medical College Hospital for an X-ray and setting in a plaster cast, but he knew that no treatment was available there. She would have to make do with our first aid.

We were trying to catch up on a little sleep when Jabbor and Nirmal woke us at 2:00 P.M. to tell us that Punjabi troops were setting up an installation of heavy stationary guns on the hillside in front of us. At 2:30 they raised the Pakistani flag high on the hill. Simultaneously two Pakistani Air Force planes flew overhead, dived, and bombed twice. Their target was the radio station on the outskirts of the city. We were concerned because this station was close to the large automobile and railway bridge on the only road between us and our hospital.

Seeing the Pakistani flag, students and other men climbed the hill to check which side was really there. Some thought it was the Bengal Regiment using the flag as a hoax; others knew by their broken speech that the men were not Bengalis.

Jabbor reminded us that those same soldiers who had been firing down on people passing in the street had been able to watch as wounded Bengali fighters came and went in our house. If those were really Punjabi troops a mere five hundred yards away, we were in danger. He felt that we should leave.

It was too late in the day to attempt a move. Reid and Nirmal walked through back lanes to Reid's house. Overhearing some Bengalis asking each other if this man was a Punjabi in plain clothes, Reid began speaking Bengali. He stopped and made conversation with every person he knew and some he didn't. He kept nonchalantly slipping in the phrase that he was an American. Finally, the tension over, neighbors vouched for his nationality. At his house, Reid checked the gas and hooked up the battery charger to his open-backed Landrover.

That evening's Bible reading came alive as we read, sitting at the bottom of an hostile hill, "Thou preparest my table before me in the presence of my enemies." And the table was well-laden, including homemade bread, with everything cooked in the Sunbeam electric frying pan.

We were able to stay in our own rooms that night, although there was much firing in the distance. But somehow we were all jumpy and restless — all of us except Reid, who during the day had patched the holes where the mosquitoes were getting in; he slept soundly.

Soon after breakfast, Reid and Jabbor set out to make arrangements for our departure. We had little money and couldn't just pull out without telling anybody where we were going. The two walked over a mile before they could find a bicycle rickshaw driver who was brave enough to drive near the area where the Punjabi troops were capturing more territory every minute.

Arriving at our Bible Information Center, they found a camp of twenty-one people who had fled from their homes. John Sircar, a young man who lives and works at the center, had assumed responsibility for the group and was trying to maintain some degree of order amid the general confusion.

John explained that some of the current pandemonium was caused because two men had left the center the previous night for the Gurganus' house and had not yet returned. John also

knew the fate of some others of our church group. Christian
nurses serving at the Medical College Hospital had left as the
Punjabi soldiers came in. Some of them, accompanied by
younger brothers, had started to walk to safety at the Chandraghona Mission Hospital in the Chittagong Hill Tracts — twenty-
five miles away.

The Bible Information Center was still in territory held by
the Bengali Liberation Army, but the Punjabi troops were
rapidly approaching it. They held the area where the Gurganuses
and the rest of the foreign community were staying. Because
of that, the nationals at our office thought it would be unsafe
for Jabbor to walk through no-man's land and straight into
Punjabi territory. Theoretically, Reid should be safe on either
side.

Leaving instructions that Jabbor should start back to the rest
of us if he did not return by noon, Reid set out walking alone.
About a half-mile down the road, he reached a major inter-
section. The Chittagong Medical College Hospital occupies one
corner, a Hindu orphanage spreads over the top of the opposite
hill, and our grocery-general store is located where the roads
converge. There, a group of the Pakistan military stopped Reid
and questioned him, then advised him to wait for an hour before
venturing further. "We have some operations to perform," was
their explanation.

A German expatriate joined Reid during the wait. He had
been in his house behind the grocery store, having been unable
to get to Dacca and the evacuation planes. He described the
fierce fighting between the Pakistan army and the Bengali
liberators which had resulted in the Pakistanis controlling all
the hilltops and the strategic buildings of the medical college.

During the wait, Reid watched the soldiers force their way
into the cluster of small shops and help themselves to what they
wanted. An Urdu-speaking man pled with them not to steal,
but they pushed him away.

When the designated hour was up, Reid started again. Arriving at the Gurganus' house and the connecting homes of
other Americans, he found twenty-six foreigners waiting for the
next development. Men were out playing catch, while the
ladies were raiding their freezers and pantries to come up with
tasty menus.

They informed Reid about what had been happening in that

part of town. He saw the shrapnel and bullets lying in the yard. Their general feeling was that the whole show was over — the Punjabis virtually had won and within a day or two everything would be under martial law control. That seemed to be a sensible conclusion. Reid decided that we would stay, and started the long walk back. Meeting up with Jabbor again, they bought some food, including a huge ripe watermelon.

But in the meantime, Lynn and I had packed up to go to Malumghat and onward if necessary. We locked all of our valuables into a drum. We sorted through and burned any papers or printed material that could in any way incriminate us. Then we considered what to take with us. Previously we had packed evacuation suitcases with slides, clothes, and souvenirs: everything we'd want to take home. We had carried those suitcases down to the Field Council meetings and brought them back with us again. This time there would be no room in the car to take suitcases. We had to save the space for people and food. We decided that Lynn and I would take one tote bag between us. We each wore two dresses and stuffed the red tote with a change of underwear, a "Sunday dress" each, a jewelry bag, a cosmetic bag, and a bag of those silly bouffant hair rollers which took up too much space. (Apparently the contents of our tote bag was the topic of much comment by the friends who read of it in our prayer letters. The idea of two girls evacuating their home with one tote bag between them!)

More important by far than what was in that little bag was the leather folder containing the precious manuscript of the Bible translation and some of the literature projects.

During the packing, two currents were whirling around us. When she realized what we were doing, the Didi-Ma flatly declared that she would not leave. She hadn't run away before and she wouldn't this time either. What could we do? We couldn't leave her, nor could we take her anywhere. Suddenly, in one of the coincidences in which God delights, her son knocked on the gate, coming to check on how we all were. Within minutes, she picked up her one other sari, tucked the cat under her arm, and with an "I told you so" look about her marched off down the road to her son's house where she lived in oblivion and safety throughout all the disturbances.

Simultaneously, our neighbors in the apartment downstairs called up to ask us what our plans were. Hearing we had a place to go, the young mother of six children, all under eight years old, burst into tears. "Take us with you, too. Please take us, too." It was heartbreaking to have to say, "There is no room," but the car was already dangerously overloaded.

Then Reid arrived at 12:30 with the bombshell that he thought we should stay put. We presented him with the reasons why we thought we should go:

— Although we weren't particularly afraid of possible death from actual direct hits, it seemed foolish to perch there like sitting ducks if there was a chance to move away.

— Reid had made the casual statement Tuesday evening that what worried him the most was what the Punjabi soldiers would do to women after they won the victory. This bothered us too — not only for ourselves, but especially for the young Boshu girls.

— We were very tired from having slept so poorly for the past five nights.

— We had run out of water again and were low on other supplies.

Reid didn't pay much attention to those arguments. Then one of us — I don't remember if it was Lynn or I — said quietly, "I think the Lord wants us to go this time."

That was enough for Reid. He'd argue with us, but he wasn't going to argue with the Lord.

In my case, this definite leading was a unique thing. My Christian experience has been one of just following along step after step. I haven't had any dramatic episodes of finding the Lord's will. Even in the big things — choosing a school, picking a field of service — the pieces have just fallen into place without voices or lights or special guidance. But this was different. It was a definite, "This is the way; walk ye in it."

Once it was decided that we would go, Reid wasted no time. After dispatching Nirmal to get Rachel Dass, he and Jabbor made their way to the car. Miraculously, it started on the first turn of the engine. Then came the dilemma: should he weave in and out of lanes where unknown dangers lurked, or should he drive on the main road directly under the sights of the heavy artillery? Reid opted for the latter.

I took one last tour around to make sure that everything

was shut and locked. I bent to check the flame of the refrigerator. For five days its tank had registered "empty." Even as I watched, the flame sputtered and died.

Mr. Dass and Rachel walked up as the car stopped at the corner of our lane. Five of us piled into the cab, and the rest squished in the back among the bags of rice, flour, and clothes. The biggest problem was the nearly flat left rear tire. We found a rickshaw willing to load in two adults, one child, and one dog; then we all limped along together until Reid could get his tire pump from our office.

With the tire pumped up and a push to get us started, we headed out of town. We weren't the only ones leaving. Vehicles of every make and vintage, crammed with people and possessions, honked their way past us, and we joined the procession.

On the outskirts of the city we passed the radio station which had been the target of shelling and strafing earlier in the week. Shortly beyond the city limits the checkpoints began. At each we were stopped, questioned, and sometimes searched. Some blockades were manned by sharp guards trained by the East Pakistan Rifles; some had attendants who looked as if they didn't know which end of the gun to hold. The most thorough check was at the big railway-car bridge. There they called Reid aside and begged him to get in touch with President Nixon. It was heartbreaking to us to realize how much faith (at that time misplaced faith) they had in our country.

Naively assuming that we would have some direct means of contacting the United States, they cried, "If America only knew what is really happening here, they would come and help us."

At one spot a man stuck his head in the window of our car and asked, "Don't you know me?"

I didn't recognize the red-shirted guard until he reminded me: he was the counter clerk who sold us our plane tickets at the PIA office.

In all, there were seventeen checkpoints in the sixty-five-mile route. At each stop we gave a donation to the Liberation Army. At the halfway point we stopped by the side of the road to uncramp and to eat the watermelon and breathe air not polluted with artillery fumes or the stench of decay.

It was hard to believe that we were fleeing a doomed city. Here, the spring afternoon was pleasant and peaceful; Bangladesh flags still adorned every doorpost; villagers still greeted one another with a "Joi Bangla!"

At 5:30 we pulled into the Memorial Christian Hospital compound. Missionary Larry Golin was walking the stretch of road between the hospital buildings and the residences.

Grinning widely as he ran over to us, he summed it all up with, "Boy, are we glad to see you!"

Driving straight back from the hospital buildings past the national staff quarters and the complex of missionary family homes, it seemed as if we had arrived at an oasis of peace. The war seemed far away. By the time we reached the nurses' home at the extreme end of the compound, word of our coming had spread. Most of the missionary family and many of our Bengali friends converged on us for a teary, joyful reunion.

Everyone started talking at once. Our Field Council chairman, Jay Walsh, suggested, "Let's have a meeting so we can all hear the same story once."

That meeting began the most meeting-filled three weeks of our lives. Every time there was a new development, every time someone was making a decision, the value of full consultation was appreciated. At that first meeting we gave the report from Chittagong.

Then — the pleasure of a full night of uninterrupted sleep. Well, not quite uninterrupted. The hospital is adjacent to a woodcutting station of reserve forest land. The logs are cut at the top of the hill and rolled down into waiting sampans. When the logs began clunking, Lynn woke with a start, thinking she was back among rifle shots again.

Lynn Silvernale (l), Jeannie, and Becky Davey (r)
at Memorial Christian Hospital

Reid Minich
on his Honda

Bullet holes in Jeannie's house

The ravages of war

ABWE Bible Information Center, Chittagong

Drs. Peter and
Reba MacField
and baby
"Bubbly"

Jabbor, his wife,
and two sons

Evacuation group in Bangkok

Front row, children seated: Amy DeCook, Susann
Beals, Kimberly Beals, David Ketcham, Timmy Golin,
Marty Ketcham, Stevie DeCook, Danny Golin

Second row, children standing: David DeCook,
Danny DeCook, Mark Olsen, Sheryl Walsh, Michelle
Beals, Shelly Walsh

Third row: Dr. Joe DeCook, Joyce DeCook, Becky
Ketcham, Marjorie Beals, Becky Davey, Joan Olsen,
Lynn Silvernale, Phillip Walsh

Fourth row: Jay Walsh, Eleanor Walsh, "Kitty"
Ketcham, Jeannie, Mel Beals, Jane Golin holding
Michael, Larry Golin, Linda Walsh, Nancy Olsen,
Debbie Walsh

To some God says "stay"
– to others "go"

5

To some God says "stay" – to others "go"

During our early days at Malumghat, discussions revolved largely around the question, "Should we evacuate, or should we remain here?"

The first of the decisions arrived at was that those whose furlough was nearly due should proceed home on the emergency craft being provided. Two couples, five children, and two single girls were to comprise this group. Setting Saturday as Departure Day, we all pitched in; washing, ironing, and packing away the accumulation of a four-year term. The plan was that this group of ours would join the foreign community in Chittagong to await the first outward-bound transportation. Reid would drive them to Chittagong. (Actually, he was eager to be on his way, remembering the people we had left behind. Also, his evacuation kit had been more meager than Lynn's and mine; he had brought only his shaving gear, his Bible, and one shirt, all tied up in a *lungi* — the garment worn by Bengali men of all classes, at least during leisure hours.)

Friday night we held a farewell party for those of our number who would be leaving the next day. While people were still gathering for the party/meeting, in walked Santosh Battacharjee, a young Hindu who teaches Bengali to our new missionaries. Santosh's family lives close to our house in Chittagong, and he had gone there to check on their situation. He had been through harrowing experiences: all his money had been stolen; he had been relieved of his watch by prowling thugs taking advantage of the abnormal conditions; he had seen a former college class-

63

mate shot down in cold blood. Now, seeing the three of us from Chittagong here at the hospital, his face broke into a grin of relief. He had visited us once during the days of siege but had been unable to return.

The day after we left our house, he told us, there had been intense fighting in our area. Our house had been hit during a bullet barrage. Fires had been set indiscriminately. Petrol depots and stations had been blown up, igniting and spreading more flames. Santosh had been concerned for our lives.

After hearing his grim tales, how could we send more people — especially small children — to sit and wait in a burning city?

Saturday afternoon, April 3, we were resting when Rachel Dass and the Boshu girls ran to tell us that Rachel's parents had arrived. We rushed to the Olsen home where an exhausted group of refugees from Chittagong awaited us. Others were still at the hospital. Dr. Olsen and I rode up and brought back our "Babla," his parents and little sister. Their story was beginning to have a familiar ring to it: bullets flying everywhere, dead lying in the street; heavy ammunition attacks from the hill above them. They had weathered it as long as they could, then headed for safety, traveling by horse cart, boat, and bus until they reached Memorial Christian Hospital. Our Chittagong refugee group was growing.

Palm Sunday 1971, we gathered in the lounge of the nurses' home to praise the One who came in the name of the Lord. The singing was superb that morning as voices blended in the harmony of praise. We were all alive and safe!

As we were leaving the worship service, Jay Walsh mentioned that he had heard a radio announcement of an evacuation ship due to leave from the port of Chittagong tomorrow or the next day.

We went back into action with the original plans. Reid didn't want to leave with the day half gone, so he instructed everyone to be ready to set off early in the morning.

About 3:30 that afternoon while Reid, Lynn, and I were discussing our Chittagong interests and making some final plans, Larry Golin burst into the room.

"I've just heard over BBC that the ship is leaving at 8:00 tomorrow morning. Everyone who wants to evacuate must be on board this evening."

Reid, who a short time before hadn't wanted to leave so late in the day (for very good reasons), now got moving. The cars were packed — our largest American flags hung on the cars — and by 4:15 they were on their way.

"Lord, *hold that sun up,*" was the fervent prayer of the entire group. But God had other plans. The little VW had trouble and needed repairs enroute. It was quite dark by the time they reached the checkpoint at Patiya, still sixteen miles south of Chittagong.

The Bengali officer there forbade them to drive further, wisely telling them, "We will respect your flag — and I think the Punjabis on the other side will, likewise, but — if they *can't see it,* what then?"

This officer directed the group to a two-room government rest house for the night, and he arranged for eggs and rice to be provided for them.

At sunrise the cars started off again. The closer they got to the city, the stronger became the smell of death and decay. Reid said he was glad that the children were familiar with the obnoxious odor of fish drying out in the sunshine. In response to their, "What's that *awful smell?*" he reminded them about the stinky *shukti-mach* — the dried fish that's such a favorite item of village Bengalis.

The cars crossed the Bengali-Punjabi lines in safety and raced through empty streets to the dock. "Will the ship be gone? Are we too late?" were the questions in everyone's mind.

"It's there! The ship's still there!"

God had bettered their prayer. Instead of holding up the sun, He had held up the ship—held its departure until the last eleven passengers could get on board. A total of 119 foreigners, 37 of them Americans, sailed away that morning on the British merchant ship, the *Clan McNaire.*

Meanwhile, a new group had arrived at Malumghat seeking haven: four national doctors from the Chittagong Medical College Hospital. Unmistakably, God had His hands on two of these doctors. We realized this later as Dr. Peter MacField shared his story with us.

"As far back as September of 1970 I knew the country was headed for trouble. Friends advised me to get out while I could.

Actually I did have an opportunity, for I was chosen out of 150 applicants for a medical fellowship in Libya. I was excited about this appointment and could not understand my mother's persistent stand that this was not God's will. She must have been right, because even though high government officials helped, I was unable to get a passport or the necessary papers to leave the country.

"I had just returned to Dacca from the family Christmas celebration, when I received a phone call from my brother telling me that my mother had died. Later we were to see God's hand in her death. She died peacefully and painlessly. Had she lived on into the war, she would have suffered, not only the mental anguish of worrying about us, but also she would have been unable to buy the medication which controlled her serious heart condition.

"On January 28, the government transferred me to the Chittagong Medical College Hospital. This was rather inconvenient since my wife Reba, a final year medical student, was still in Dacca, 175 miles away. As tension mounted during February and March, I decided that Reba had to join me in Chittagong; whatever happened, at least we would be together. After numerous futile attempts to get to the capital city, I finally joined her on March 10. Her final exams were set for March 28. I could understand how she felt as we left Dacca, knowing that she was postponing—who could say for how long—her dream of finishing medical school.

"I continued working at the hospital. My department is cancer research and radiotherapy, but with the riots and the slaughter going on throughout the city, and especially in the dock area as the *Swat* ship unloaded, I spent a lot of time in the Emergency Room.

"As we went to bed on March 26, I confessed to Reba that I was feeling uneasy and gloomy. I explained to her that if any firing sounded nearby, she should slip off the bed onto the floor. At 10:00 P.M. the shooting started.

"The two of us and our family helper and friend, Sylvester, crawled under the dining room table and spent the rest of the night there. In the morning we realized our precarious position. We were at the end of a road only two hundred yards away from a military camp. Bullets from both sides were shooting over, around, and through our house. The area where we lived was one of the hardest hit in the city. On the corner just beyond our house, seven thousand people were killed indiscriminately. One man lived to crawl out among the corpses left to rot in the open drains along the sides of the road. He was found days later, an emotional and physical wreck.

"We took what food and clothes we could carry and headed for the Medical College. The three of us moved into the radio therapy office and set up housekeeping. We tried to maintain some semblance of medical care for the patients left in the hospital. Almost all of the nurses had left; only five doctors remained. We had no food, no electricity, no water. There was no dearth of medicine, but there was a dearth of hands to administer anything other than the most superficial care.

"As long as I live I will remember the expression on the face of a father as he looked at me through his glazed eyes. 'I'll give you any amount of money you ask for,' he gasped. 'Just save my children.' The three youngsters lying on the stretchers next to his were already dead.

"One old man was dying. He called out for a drink, but we didn't have a drop of water in the entire seven-storied, five hundred-bed hospital. I opened a bottle of sterile IV fluid and gave him his last drink.

"The Bengali Regiment were bravely trying to hold their strategic spots on the tops of the hills. The lights went out during the night of March 28. During those hours of darkness, the Pakistani military entered the city in force. Some rode in commandeered trucks; some crawled through the drains. In the face of this strength of numbers and superior arms and ammunition, the Bengalis had to retreat.

"Much against my better judgment, Reba insisted that she had to have a bath. The nurses' residence, about a quarter mile away, still had water in its tanks. While she was there, a furious barrage of shelling hit the hospital and the very building where she was bathing. Reba, under the force of the water faucet and her happiness to be clean again, didn't even hear the shelling going on around her. The few girls who were left in the building banged on the bathroom door as they fled. She dressed quickly and started to run back to where I was. I watched her stumble and lose her shoes as she ran, and gratefully pulled her, barefooted, to safety.

"With the Bengali resistance broken, the Pakistani military

grew bolder. One captain marched into the hospital, beat up a a menial worker, and announced, 'If I find any ammunition here, I will blow up the hospital and shoot everyone.'

"Another soldier, a captain, stepped up to one of the top floor windows for target practice. Getting a pedestrian in his sights, he would say, 'Fall,' and his weapon would crackle. I expected at any moment to hear that fatal 'Fall' directed at me.

"On March 31 we were eating in the doctor's hostel on the far side of the main building. Returning to the lobby of the hospital, we heard the stomping of boots overhead. Suddenly we came upon a sentry with his gun pointed at us. 'We heard firing coming from this building. We're going to search thoroughly,' he explained.

"We were marched up the stairs and confined in a private room. We had committed no crime; we were guilty of nothing but our mother tongue. We were Bengalis!

"A captain and a number of his lackies pushed into the room. In their tour of the hospital, they had come upon a Bihari patient who claimed that his bandage had not been changed for five days. The captain was infuriated that we should treat an Urdu-speaking person with such disrespect. He turned on us with his gun. One of his own countrymen, a West Pakistani medical student, pled with him: 'There are only five doctors in the whole building! They couldn't possibly have time to tend to such a minor matter as changing a bandage.' The captain paid no attention to this logic. Raising his gun, he said, 'You will all die!'

"In that split second a guard who had been posted at the veranda lookout ran in shouting, 'Come quick! We've spotted a Bengal Regiment soldier.' The captain took off like a shot. His men followed him. (Some wanted to get into the action, but others were more interested in sneaking away for a four o'clock cup of tea.) Suddenly it dawned on me that *they had all gone!* They hadn't left even one soldier to guard us.

"Without hesitation we ran down the steps, out of the building, and through a seldom-used gate into the late afternoon shadows. We didn't stop running until we reached a friend's house in the part of the city that was still in Bengali hands. And even that was just an overnight stop. Early the next morning Sylvester, Reba and I, and two Muslim doctors fled from the city. Arriving in the town of Patiya, I had it in mind to keep right on going to India. Thousands were crossing the border daily. I had helped out in relief medical work before; I could be of help in one of the camps. But Reba, who was three months' pregnant at the time, had had enough. She didn't want to run anymore.

"'I know a girl from my home church who works at the Memorial Christian Hospital,' she said, 'Let's go there. I'm sure they'll take us in.'

"I was a little skeptical, not only at the thought of complete strangers welcoming us, but also at the idea of the 'Christian' part. Oh, of course, I was a Christian. I was born into a Christian family. But the long years of study had broadened my outlook. I now felt that if you were a student of the Bible, then you would believe the Bible; but if you were a student of science, you would believe in Science. The thought of moving in with people who were probably convinced that the Bible was true did not appeal to me, but I realized that I couldn't push Reba any further.

"We arrived at Memorial Christian Hospital in Malumghat late Sunday afternoon, April 4. We need not have worried about the welcome. Reba met her friend, and Miss Becky Davey, the hospital matron, did the rest. She found places for us to live. She took care of our household needs. She provided saris, blouses, petticoats, and shoes for my wife. She is a most wonderful person.

"As far as the religious side went, we teamed up in our exile with the Dass family. They didn't force their rather straight-laced views of God and the Bible on me; they lived Christ. They encouraged me to pray with them. I decided to experiment with this praying business with all my heart. I would let God show me who He is and what He could do."

You will meet Dr. Peter again.

You can't put
your radio station here

6

You can't put
your radio station here

With our first batch of missionaries safely out of the country, we began to finalize evacuation plans for the rest of us should it become necessary. Out of our multiplicity of meetings came these four possibilities:

1. Those who wished to leave would be taken to Chittagong in hopes that there would be another air or sea lift.
2. A truck would be hired to drive the ninety miles to Teknaf, the border point between Pakistan and Burma. From there we would cross the Naf River and proceed by bus to the Burmese city of Akjab.
3. In the event the overland route proved impossible, we would hire sampans or launches to take us directly from our hospital dock to Akjab.
4. We would take a sampan or launch out toward Chittagong or wherever we heard of a rescue ship in the Bay of Bengal.

All of these ideas had their drawbacks. We were dealing with a group of twenty-two adults and twenty-five children. The truck trip was a bare possibility, but the thought of taking these twenty-five children on a five-day "cruise" squatting in a round-bottomed sampan was more of a nightmare than anyone cared to imagine.

We formed a committee to work out actual details of the various tentative options. We dubbed this "The Panic Committee." They did a good job rounding up duffle bags, canteens, tinned food, and water jugs. Seven years before, during the construction phase of our hospital, our builders Paul Goodman and

Tom McDonald, World War II men, had brought out tins of K
rations. These were added to our emergency supplies.

Our whole group was divided into three sections, trying to
equally distribute little children, older children, medical personnel, new missionaries, and old-timers. The sections were
distinguished by red, blue, and yellow ribbons. (The yellow
group complained that they had a strike against them before
the plan was even tried!)

While making our own preparations, we carefully tried to urge
our national staff and the Chittagong refugees to think out a
plan of escape. They falsely believed that as long as we were
there nothing would happen to them.

"And what will you do if the military arrive and start shooting?" we asked.

"Oh, we'll just all run to your houses," they answered naively.

Good Friday night—or really at 3:00 A.M.—Becky and Lynn
were awakened by the sound of a car driving around the house.
They cautiously made their way to the screen door and listened
as the car circled the family housing area. Within a few minutes,
Jay Walsh drove up on his cycle with his hand resting on his
gun. The night air carried his voice to where the girls were
standing.

"This is a *hospital;* we are doctors here," Jay was saying.

The mystery was solved the next morning. The car had been
full of Awami League leaders who wanted to set up the Free
Bangladesh Radio Station on our hospital property. They had
looked the place over and decided that the nurses' home was the
most unobstructed building. They would take part of it over,
thank you very much.

The four missionary men who met with the Awami League
leaders had tried to talk them out of the idea, but they were
insistent. Jay was sure they would be back, so we met together
to discuss this problem. We all felt that we should absolutely
forbid them to set up the station on our property, unless, of
course, they took it over by force. We would compromise with
them and give them a small portable generator which they could
attach to their vehicle and use to broadcast clandestinely from
the depths of the jungle.

Jay had been right. The men did return. First they came in
the early evening with an electrical engineer whom they were
holding under arrest. They asked us to decide this matter in

their favor and left. At 9:30 they were back again. While Dr. Olsen and Jay Walsh met with the men, the rest of us prayed and sang prayer songs. Does God answer prayer? Jay and Vic Olsen walked in with their faces beaming. The men had abandoned the idea of using the hospital for their radio base. They realized that the radio frequency would be easy to pick up and the enemy would be ruthless in bombing such a site. That was the last we heard of project radio.

Easter Sunday, 1971—The day began with a sunrise service at 6:00 A.M. Throughout the day there were services and classes helping us to commemorate the high point of the Christian faith. At the close of an afternoon ladies' Bible class, a car full of Awami League leaders pulled into the hospital. Jumping out quickly, they told their tale. Captain Haroon, one of the highest ranking officers in the Liberation Army, had been seriously wounded in heavy fighting near the railway-car bridge just on the outskirts of Chittagong. They had taken him to their field hospital in Patiya where doctors had performed abdominal surgery. Working without anesthesia, with merely a shot of Demerol as a pain-killer, they had removed two feet of bowel laced with bullets. Now they declared, "He is in a very weak condition from losing so much blood."

Within minutes, laboratory technologist Bob Adoph drew blood from one of the men in the car, and they tore back up the road with it. Dr. Donn Ketcham advised that they get the captain out of his temporary surroundings and bring him to the hospital. A few days later they brought this desperately sick man to us. Repair surgery was performed, and he convalesced posing as a bank manager from Chittagong. Before the Pak military actually did arrive on the hospital property looking for him, Dr. Ketcham had arranged for his transfer to a safe area.

During those days Lynn and I felt a particular responsibility for our Chittagong refugees. We scavenged in the remains of the missionaries' gardens, picking beans and green vegetables. (Did you know that old, bitter lettuce cooks up quite well?) We would march up to the refugees' homes each morning carrying baskets of produce to divide among them. We also tried to keep tabs on the children. All this free space to run in! And those bicycles to ride! It was too much temptation for city kids, especially those who had been housebound during the weeks of unsettled conditions.

During most of our time there, Lynn worked on the missionaries' language program and helped in the hospital. My time was filled with teaching first and second grades for the missionary kids who had lost their teacher and writing material for our annual Children's Camp.

We also helped fill the time by keeping up a "journal" just in case we ever would want to recall or tell other people about the events of those days. Here is how that journal reads:

Friday, April 16 — 2:20 P.M.

Everyone was enjoying an afternoon nap, when suddenly the cry went up, "The military have come." Families from up on the hospital property, household servants, and other workers began swarming back to the houses. We learned that both Patiya and Amirabad (45 and 25 miles from Malumghat, respectively) had been bombed. Actually there were no troops coming down the road yet.

We met to discuss what to do in the event of bombing at Malumghat. Decision: Head for the jungle and get into the World War II trenches still there. Mel Beals was assigned to locate and clean out trenches. Lynn and I were to "plane watch" from the roof of the nurses' residence. A gong is to be sounded when a plane is spotted.

We had just finished eating dinner when Reid Minich arrived with three American men.

Another meeting at 8:15!

The three were: an economic advisor with the U.S. Consulate and two A.I.D. men from Dacca. The four had come from Chittagong in the Gurganus' VW bus and Jeep station wagon, with our two big American flags flying.

They had come to give us the strongest warning to leave the country that the U.S. Government ever gives to private citizens. They said that it had been announced over VOA the evening before that Americans in Chittagong District should leave via Burma. None of us had heard that announcement. (We had been in a meeting!)

We asked the men many questions. Much of their information was encouraging. They didn't feel that we were in danger of actual fighting at the hospital unless the Awami League took it over and put up resistance. They felt that the nationals on the property were safe as long as we were there. Only the

Hindus were in real danger. The men left it up to us to make our decision as to who would leave the country. They were to return to Chittagong at 11:00 A.M. the next day. They wanted to go to the military authorities to get them to stop the bombing and strafing for a couple of days in order to allow us to pass through the area to safety. The plan was for a convoy of American cars to take us to Chittagong where the missionaries would board a STOL or larger plane for Dacca.

When the discussion of the evacuation plans was over for the night and most of the group had gone to pray and make their private decisions, Lynn and I stayed on and urged Reid to clue us in on what had been happening in Chittagong in the days since we had left. His account was not encouraging.

"The day I took the bunch of missionaries to the ship," Reid said, "I met a U.S. A.I.D. man on the dock. He mentioned that there were foreigners stranded up at Kaptai (where the Americans built a dam in the early 1960s). He asked if there was a Bengali national who could accompany him, as he didn't speak the language.

"'If it's someone to speak *Bengali* you want, I'll go with you,' I volunteered.

"The A.I.D. man agreed at once. Foreseeing danger in this trip, I suggested we pray before starting. I recall his commenting, 'It's good to pray again.' (He had been witnessed to by a Campus Crusade worker).

"The first problem was to get gasoline for the car. Petrol was strictly rationed. Only the military were allowed to pull up to a pump and say, 'Fill her up.' Hunting for a station, we drove through streets where everything was in flames.

"Out on the road toward Kaptai we passed the damaged and captured radio station. In another hundred yards we were abreast of Pakistani tanks which had only minutes before ceased firing in the very direction we had to proceed. The road was covered with freshly spent shell casings. A line of twenty or twenty-five Bengalis, hands over their heads, was being marched down the road. After passing the second tank and becoming quite uncomfortable with their gun muzzles pointing over our heads, we checked with an officer for permission to continue on our way. He told us, 'We're still clearing out this area,' and sent us back to the radio station to wait for a half hour.

"When permission finally came to pass through no man's land, we were told, 'Go quickly through this area. We cannot tell when firing will break out again. And one last word of warning: *do not come back after dark*. If you cannot return before dusk, wait until tomorrow morning.'

"People of various nationalities were waiting to be rescued from Kaptai. As we loaded them into the cars, I realized that one family, Americans, were holding back. Taking me inside, they disclosed that they were sheltering a West Pakistani family, and they asked if I would hide these people among the boxes and bedding and take them out to safety.

"Bengalis were in control of the Kaptai area, and it was a sure thing that if foreigners left, this West Pak family was dead! I sympathized with the Americans' attitude. There are always good people on both sides of enemy lines. We, too, had friends among the West Pak community. I knew that the only way I could stay alive through all of this was to keep all of my dealings open and aboveboard. I couldn't jeopardize my chance of helping our own missionaries and nationals by being party to deceit.

"Seeing no other possibility, this family elected to stay on and save the lives of their friends. It was a courageous decision.

"The Bengali forces, knowing that the Pakistani family was being sheltered there, suspected trickery. They gave those cars a most thorough inspection. We couldn't have concealed a mouse!

"As soon as the Pakistan military took over Kaptai, my A.I.D. friend returned to assist that one remaining American family. They had safely turned over their Pakistani 'house guests' to the military and were free to evacuate with a clear conscience. But by then the tables had turned; now it was the Bengalis who needed protection. The two Americans risked their lives in an unsuccessful attempt to protect a Bengali engineer, one of the top men on the Kaptai Dam project, when he was forcibly taken by the military. Having been ordered at gun point to get back into the house, the two men had to obey. A few seconds later, only a hundred yards from the house, a crazed Pakistani major gave the order and the Bengali engineer fell to the ground in a pool of blood. He died instantly. This Bengali had personally seen to the safety of half a dozen West Pakistani families during their days of fear and danger, but no one could protect him from a Pakistani major gone mad with hate."

After listening to Reid's disquieting report, we were sober as we went to our room to weigh the issue again: "Should we evacuate or should we stay?"

Saturday, April 17—We met as a group this morning. Sitting in a circle, we reported what we had decided. Such difficult, soul-searching decisions! No one wanted to split up families, but many felt it was wrong to keep the children in a place of possible danger and privation.

An hour was spent in discussing the pros and cons of staying or going.

Lynn and I, independently, had decided that the Lord was leading us to stay on and "redeem the time": each extra day meant getting the already prepared Bible translation and litera-ture material more nearly into usable form. As I wrote home, "Please be assured we are not trying to be heroes; we are not out to make martyrs. We do have an evacuation route planned, and if God says 'Go,' we'll move out *quick*. We just don't have the green light as of now."

Some of our group felt that their ministry would be severely hampered during these troubled days, so why should they stay on, using up the dwindling supply of food and other needed commodities?

Those of us who did not have valid East Pakistan return visas feared that if we were to leave we would not be permitted to reenter the country.

We learned that the Americans had had an interesting talk with Awami leaders the night before. The nationals had con-ducted themselves in a fine manner. They knew what they were fighting for and what the consequences would be. The Ameri-cans made it very clear that the U.S. was not in a position to recognize Bangladesh nor to send in help. The Awami leaders were in dire straits. They had lost their homes and posses-sions: many had not heard of the fate of their families.

Sunday, April 18

After English church service, the decision as to who would leave was reviewed again. The Beals had decided that rather than Marjorie and the children going on the evacuation, the whole family would take their vacation in Penang, going via Burma.

In the afternoon Reid arrived by motorcycle. He said that conditions in the city were worsening rapidly: utter lawlessness, looting, occasional gunfire—a highly tense atmosphere. He made the comment that having been at Malumghat where everything was so peaceful, he had wondered if it were really necessary for people to leave, but after returning to Chittagong he knew that now was the time to get out.

Everybody helped the evacuees pack.

Becky and Lynn devised a code of Bible verses which everyone would take along so that we could communicate with each other safely.

Acts 16:7	—We are trying to get back but are unable to.
2 Kings 7:7	—All missionaries are out except for the three men who must stay.
2 Kings 7:10b	—Everybody out—even the three men.
2 Kings 4:2	—Food shortage and other problems making reentry not advisable.
Isaiah 30:15	—All clear. Come back.
Jeremiah 4:1a	—Come back. You are needed.
Genesis 28:21	—West Pak group is going home.
Acts 21:4	—Don't come back yet.
Acts 16:36	—Military have sent us out safely.

Monday, April 19

The plane evacuation group, the Adolph family with their four children and five women missionaries, left at 8:00 A.M. in two Landrovers driven by Larry Golin and Dr. Joe DeCook. Reid went on ahead on his cycle.

Along the way they met a British man who was to have come to Malumghat for treatment. He hadn't shown up, and we had assumed he had gone out on the evacuation ship. Actually he had taken refuge in villages on the way to the hospital. He was so happy to see white faces, and he eagerly hopped into one of the cars to join the evacuees. Soon, however, they met a car flying a huge Union Jack—Britishers out scouting for this man. He switched cars and went on under the protection of his own flag.

At the broken bridge, our people walked across to where cars awaited them on the other side. They saw dead bodies that had been left where they had fallen. Multiple holes in the buildings revealed the heavy strafing in the area.

Arriving safely in Chittagong, this group went on by plane to Dacca and then either to West Pakistan or to their homes in the U.S.

The departing missionaries had had no time to sort and put away their belongings, so some of us spent the day cleaning up. Some of the families had sent over boxes of children's clothes for Lynn and me to distribute to our refugees. This set us off on a long-delayed project: the drums of used clothing in the hospital storage area, clothes no one ever had had the time to sort out. We had these delivered to the nurses' residence, and soon we had a grand array of shirts, shoes, dresses, and baby clothes spread all over the veranda.

Tuesday, April 20

Jay Walsh and Joe DeCook drove the Beals family to Teknaf to get them on their way through Burma. On the way back the two men met with fresh roadblocks, unsmiling guards, and evidence that there would be heavy resistance in this area.

The new "Panic Committee" met. (All the former members had left!) We — Vic and Joan Olsen, Eleanor Walsh, and I — set up a suggested program that we called "Village Haven."

If the troops came, at the sound of firing from the hospital area (half a mile from the missionary residences), all women and children and an assigned male leader would head for our friends' houses in the nearby village. We could take food, water, first aid supplies, and lightweight games to help pass the time. We didn't expect to have to stay there for long.

But that was before Becky Davey "made her first medical mistake"!

The flight
from Malunghat

7

The flight
from Malumghat

As long as there is a Memorial Christian Hospital at Malumghat, Bangladesh, the tale will be told of Becky Davey's "first medical mistake."

What was this historic mistake made by the efficient Director of Nursing? Somehow she had forgotten to tell Dr. Donn Ketcham about a patient who very obviously needed surgery. By the time the national nurses realized this and the surgery got underway, it was 9:15 P.M. When Becky returned from surgery, keyed up and not ready to go to bed, she turned on the radio — something she rarely does. She couldn't tune in Voice of America at first, but picked it up just as they were giving the summary of news at 11:15. Becky listened to the summary — then —

> "Now a special announcement for the Americans at Malumghat. The U.S. government strongly advises all but essential personnel to proceed immediately by motor vehicle to the Burma border. The Chittagong exit is no longer available . . . REPEAT — "The U.S. government strongly advises. . . ."

It was months later that Reid told us the background of that announcement.

"When the airlift evacuation group saw the ravaged city of Chittagong, they were badly shaken and insisted, '*All* our people must vacate the country.'

"Then to our horror we learned that the British Baptist Hospital at Chandraghona, twenty-five miles from the city, had been raked with machine gun fire without any warning whatsoever. Their leprosy hospital had been hit by a rocket and one patient killed. The Chandraghona people had felt secure, that nothing would be done without the military giving them sufficient warning. Their trust had been misplaced.

"As soon as the Pakistan military arrived at the hospital, they made a bed-to-bed search for wounded guerrilla fighters. To further terrorize the hospital staff, they marched a group of Bengalis onto the hospital compound and shot them in cold blood in front of the hospital building.

"The brigadier in Chittagong would give no guarantee for the safety of our people at Memorial Christian Hospital. If the Mukti Bahini made a stand at the hospital, the Pakistan military would attack them on that very spot.

"This was shattering news. It must be relayed to Malumghat without delay. Our people must be gotten out of the hospital compound. But how to get the word to them? Chandraghona had received no warning before attack; Malumghat was equally endangered. Captain Haroon was a patient at Malumghat!

"There was only one way — the Voice of America radio. Arrangements had been made that they would give vital messages to our group of missionaries at 7:00 A.M. and 7:00 P.M. when the situation called for it. Now was the time. The only catch was that VOA didn't *know* the present danger to our Malumghat people. The A.I.D. man and I got our heads together and prepared a message. It was then 4:00 P.M. Amazingly, he was able to get a flight to Dacca. He transmitted the message to Washington, and they in turn beamed back that very night:

"... Now a special announcement for the Americans at Malumghat. ..."

Becky ran to alert all of us. We gathered at the Walshes and listened to the midnight news, but there was no repeat announcement then. For the first time in all of our deliberations, everyone seemed to be agreed that we should heed this advice and head for Burma. The possibility of going to Hebron, our jungle station, was dismissed and rejected.

The final decision was for Dr. Vic Olsen and Dr. Donn Ketcham to stay and all others (totaling twenty-nine) to leave.

This was put down as an official record. In the absence of the others, Vic was elected Field Council Chairman and Donn was elected Secretary. The DeCooks, who had just attended their required two Field Council Meetings, were eligible to vote for the first time!

Everyone went back home to pack. Amazingly, the electricity that always died out between 10:00 and 12:00 P.M. stayed on until almost 4:00 A.M., by which time we were all packed (even all those used clothes on the veranda).

Wednesday, April 21

Up at the crack of dawn to get ready. Did anyone sleep? The same announcement was repeated on the 7:00 A.M. VOA broadcast. We had made arrangements with the men from Dacca that all messages to us should come on at 7:00 A.M. or 7:00 P.M. The fact that the announcement first came on at 11:00 P.M. signified its urgency. We finally pulled away from Malumghat at 9:00 A.M.

It was hard to leave, as the nationals were dreadfully upset. Some seemed to understand that we should go, but felt as if the bottom had dropped out of their world. So many had had their faith in us rather than in the Lord. Perhaps God moved us out to convince them to get away from us to a safer place. They would have stayed as long as we did. Some gave indication that they would head for Hebron. Others wanted to try to get shelter in Burma or even in India.

One touching moment came when the West Pakistani watchmen, whom we had been hiding from the Bengali fury, raised their closed curtain and gave the greeting *"nomaskar"* to the cars moving out.

I'll never forget one of our Chittagong teenagers, Babla. He didn't know quite what to do. Was he still a little boy who could reach out and touch me as I leaned from the car to say good-by, or was he a big boy who now must stand distant and proper? In months to come we were to learn that our Babla was no mere boy; he was a strong, courageous man.

We traveled in three Landrovers. It was sprinkling rain when we left and really began to pour before we reached Teknaf. The weepy skies reflected our own emotions that morning. But actually the clouds and the rain made it cooler; otherwise it would have been unbearably hot with so many people in each vehicle.

Eleanor Walsh said, "The Lord provided the electricity at night and the shelter from the sun in the daytime: our own pillar of fire and pillar of cloud."

There was a barricade across the road at the turnoff to the road to Burma outside of Cox's Bazar. The roadblock was chained down and the key to unlock it was with a man in Cox's. Jay went off to get it while the rest of us took a coffee break. We hunted for sugar, but none was available. A shopkeeper gave us some crude molasses free of charge.

We enjoyed the beautiful scenery on the way down to Teknaf. At Teknaf we had a three-hour wait for the tide to come in before the sampan could go, so we sat on the verandah of a group of closed shops and opened our knapsacks. We ate pork and beans, vienna sausages, bread with honey butter, and some chocolate candy from the K rations.

The men loaded the luggage onto the sampan, and we twenty-nine crammed onto the bare bamboo slats on the bottom of the boat. The boat trip was supposed to take one and a half hours, but actually stretched into three and a half, for the six miles across the Naf River from Teknaf to Maungdaw, Burma. As we pulled out of the creek into the river, we passed a sign Teknaf/BOP (Border of Pakistan).

There was a good wind, so the crew tried putting up a sail. On the first attempt one of the ropes broke, but Girl Scout Joan Olsen knotted the ropes for them and they were successful the second time. The sailing went faster, but still it was a long trip. Several times we were told to sit down so that we couldn't be seen from the checkpoints along the border. When it got dark, they told us to be quiet (impossible!) so that we wouldn't arouse the suspicion of the border guards. That would result in the boatman having to pay bigger bribes.

We docked at the Maungdaw checkpoint about 7:30 P.M. and disembarked by stepping out onto a smaller sampan, walking on its roof, and then jumping onto a slippery mud bank. All landed safely. Then we discovered that the Olsens' deputation slides had spent the three hours' travel time in the water at the bottom of the sampan. We all piled into an open bamboo house out over the water. We fed the kids peanut butter, bread, raisins, and water. A big dog kept coming in to get in on the goodies too. At last they led us off to a guest house (Dak bungalow).

There we discovered the whole Beals family; they had been detained, waiting for clearance from Rangoon for them to be able to leave. They were not especially surprised to see us. They'd had a feeling that we would be along.

Now there were thirty-four of us. Also in the same guest house were some Awami leaders who had fled East Pakistan and wanted to get to the Indian High Commissioner in Rangoon, hoping for political asylum. There were three rooms for us to use with a total of six single beds *(charpoys)*. The men and boys slept in one room. Mark Olsen used his tennis shoes for a pillow, and Joe DeCook used a roll of toilet paper. Halfway through the night, Mel Beals got cold and took down a pair of the door curtains, wrapped up in them and went to sleep. Tiny girls and their mothers were in one room, and older girls in the other.

Thirteen-year-old Becky Ketcham thought the military had come and were torturing her. She kept saying, "Ouch, Ouch!" all night. In the morning she discovered that she had covered up with an unfinished dress that still had pins in it. Fortunately there were no rats or mosquitoes — and the bats stayed out of doors. The main inconvenience was that it was cold!

Thursday, April 22

We had to have permission from Rangoon allowing us to proceed. It was providential that the Beals had gone on ahead so that these arrangements could be made. Everyone had to fill out immigration and currency forms. That finished, all thirty-four of us piled into two trucks and drove sixteen miles to Buthidaung. Those wooden seats were hard!

We drove through beautiful country. Especially interesting were the tunnels that had been used during World War II. At Buthidaung we ate peanut butter or Cheese Whiz sandwiches, using the back of the truck as counter and table. Before we finished eating, we were ushered onto an ancient patrol boat.

We had been joined on the trucks by a couple of men in army uniforms toting semi-automatics. These guards went aboard the river patrol boat with us too. The boat had an upper compartment where the luggage was stored and a tiny, hot hold. We all started out down there and finished up the sandwiches and bananas. By rearranging the luggage we saw that most people could sit up on the upper deck.

The boat trip was supposed to take eight hours. That would get us into Akyab about 9:00 P.M. Along with us, our armed guards, and the boat crew were two immigration officers and a woman whose official position we never figured out. These were an official escort assigned to see us to our destination.

The river trip was scenic, much like steamer travel in East Pakistan. For supper we ate *cold* Dinty Moore Beef Stew. Some ate it out of the vienna sausage tins saved from the first meal and others ate from the stew tins. The crew boiled water for tea and coffee for us.

At about 6:30 we stopped at a riverside village. We couldn't leave the boat, but the whole village must have come to watch us. At 9:00 P.M. we were still sailing. At first Jay told us there would be another ten-mile truck ride after we got off the boat; then he came back to say that we couldn't get off that night. By then we knew it. We kept getting stuck in sandbars and running aground. The boatmen couldn't find the right channel in the dark. They tried to get the boat turned around and really got into open rocky water.

When the kids started complaining, Eleanor said philosophically, "We're all in the same boat! But that's always the way it is when we evacuate." For sleeping, the downstairs people spread out a plastic sheet and laid all the little kids on it. The women sat around on the bench and got a chance to lie down one at a time. Those below couldn't get to the one bathroom, so they used a cracker tin with a *lungie* wrapped around for privacy. Meanwhile, up on the deck, the suitcases were spread relatively flat. People tried to stretch out, but nearly froze. Becky Ketcham dug into all the Murree winter clothes to find things to cover people up with. One of the men slept on a ledge; another slept in two tires. Jay and Mark were right outside on the rolling deck. Brr! Jane Golin had just gotten comfortable when her husband stepped on her!

Friday, April 23

At dawn, the boatmen began to pull up the anchor. Baby Michael Golin woke up with a bright smile, and the sunrise was gorgeous. The boatmen worked to pole us around an island corner, but made little progress. Jay, Mel, and Joe found a huge stick and began to pole with it. We weren't far from the stream leading to Akyab, but then we learned that the engine was unable to work. Something was wrong with the battery, and the rudder was broken. The boatmen again tried to get us around the island to where there was a house with a phone to call for help. Instead, we ran aground on a completely isolated beach. We tried to hail sampans nearby by calling and blowing the horn, but to no avail.

There was no real food left, so we opened the K ration tins and fed everyone malt tablets and pemmican. It worked — no one starved.

The crew put down a gangplank, and our guards went off to get a sampan and help. We were concerned about food for lunch. We asked the boat people to cook rice for us, but they said they didn't have any. Then we asked them to go to a village and buy some, and they refused to do that. Finally Jay hailed a sampan on the far side of the beach and went off to a village.

Our beached boat was rocking badly, and the water looked inviting, so all the kids and many others went for a swim. That was the kids' first bath since Malumghat. We had a nice morning playing on the beach.

The immigration officers woke up from quite a long sleep and asked for Jay. When they learned that he had gone to the bazaar, they were furious. They told us how dangerous it was, that there were armed Communist guerrillas in the area, and besides they were responsible for our food. Ha! We watched them eating rice and curry when we had nothing.

Almost simultaneously, our armed guards came back in the sampan with a P.T. boat following them, and Mel spotted Jay returning from the bazaar. He brought a huge stalk of bananas and bags of flaky pastry-like stuff. People in the bazaar had been very friendly to him — he had had two cups of tea.

By that time our old boat was high and dry — the tide was out. We sent the luggage and the people out to the P.T. boat in two little sampans that had to make the trip three times. How those sampans rocked with the waves. Ugh!

The men on the P.T. boat were pleasant. They even served tea (all out of one or two cups). We traveled about forty minutes on the P.T. boat; then our guard and Madame X got off onto another sampan. The P.T. boat went five minutes further, then stopped at the mouth of a creek. Several sampans began rowing toward us. We were dismayed at the thought of another sampan ride, but discovered that we were at Akyab and these were just taking us to the pier. There on the pier were two *Americans* to meet us — an Air Force attaché, Colonel Walsh, and an embassy man, Mr. Martin. We went to the Immigration building, where the men passed out American canned soft drinks to everybody.

Colonel Walsh and Mr. Martin commented that they had never seen people in our situation so well organized and so calm.

"They were actually singing as they rode in," one remarked to another of the personnel. And what had we been singing? What else but —

> "With Christ in the vessel
> We can smile at the storm."

From that point on, things began to improve. Once again we piled into trucks, and off we went to the Roman Catholic mission in Akyab, where there was one lone missionary, Father Bloom. He had been in Burma for twenty-eight years and had not left for the past ten years. If he left, he would never be able to come back. He had expected us the night before and had prepared beds for us. But at that point we were mostly interested in showers. Oh, the layers of dirt! It was good to get out of those clothes. There was a variety of food available: beef stew, fish curry, vegetables, Spam, hash — and what did the kids eat? Bread and peanut butter!

Jay and Mel were detained by the Burmese Intelligence Department who wanted all the information they could get. We rushed through eating and cleaning up and got into trucks that would take us to Akyab Airport. There, a special plane had been chartered for us — Union of Burma Airways Viscount to Rangoon.

In Rangoon we were met by more embassy people who took care of the red tape. The airlines' bus took us to the Inya Lake Hotel. The embassy assigned us rooms and had the snack bar opened for us. One of the American ladies passed out comic books to the kids who promptly lined up on the stairway and read. It sure was nice to have a hot bath and a real bed!

Jay was up until midnight talking with the American ambassador, Mr. Hummel.

Saturday, April 24

Word came through that there had been heavy firing in the area south of Chittagong. We all met with the ambassador to discuss our situation. We learned that according to the Pakistan government we had left illegally, and were advised by the American Ambassador in Islamabad, West Pakistan, *not* to try to re-enter Pakistan via Karachi at this time. We also learned that we were an embarrassment to the Burmese government, which was neutral; they hoped we would leave soon. After discussion, we agreed to leave Burma on Monday, to stay together as a group, not to make any statement to the press, but to try to get back into Pakistan as soon as possible.

We were advised to remain as inconspicuous as possible. A separate dining room had been arranged for us, and we were to pose as American tourists returning to Bangkok, Thailand.

Sunday, April 25

The kids went to the American club swimming pool. We adults toured the Schwedagon Pagoda — oh, the burning feet! Various American families in Rangoon took our families out to eat or home for fun and fellowship. In the evening a group attended the Immanuel Baptist Church in downtown Rangoon. It was noisy and difficult to hear the speaker, but the music was good.

Adhering to our promise that we would maintain the appearance of being traveling Americans, we lined up to sign the guest book, using our U.S. addresses. Thirteen-year-old Mark Olsen hollered up the line, "Hey, Mom! How do you spell Milwaukee?"

Monday, April 26

Ambassador and Mrs. Hummel, as well as other embassy personnel, were at the airport to wish us "bon voyage." "Have a good flight to Bangkok."

Imagine our joy and surprise when Rev. Bill Carlson, manager of the Christian and Missionary Alliance Guest House, stepped out of the crowd in the huge Bangkok airport. He had a truck and two VW buses lined up to take us to the guest house.

At the lovely guest house Bonnie Carlson greeted us kindly as she settled all of us into our rooms. We were no longer refugees; we were really American tourists.

Later that evening Bonnie called us aside and said, "I've taken three other groups through evacuation from their adopted land: one from Vietnam, one from Cambodia, one from Laos. I know that you are under more of a strain than you realize. I want to suggest that you take advantage of all the cultural and scenic enjoyment that Bangkok has to offer."

We took her up on the idea and went on sightseeing trips and enjoyed a variety of diversions. Of course, the biggest attraction was the shopping, especially for Lynn and me. We had a good excuse: to replace most of the things we had not been able to put in that tote bag.

Returning from one shopping expedition, I received the happy news that a phone call had come from my family, and that they would be placing it again within an hour. It was wonderful to be able to assure them that we were all safe, for communication had been impossible for many weeks.

The Carlsons outdid themselves in making things easy for us. They planned exceptionally good meals and provided transportation and information. They put up with the restlessness of twenty-one youngsters — and the perhaps equally restless thirteen adults. In fact, since confession is good for the soul, I must admit that the only window broken during our weeks at the guest house was broken by *me!* I was trying to get a little more air and forced one too hard and — splat!

Communication from our own mission, the Association of Baptists (ABWE), was waiting for us in Bangkok. The mission leaders and staff were a great encouragement. We received many cables and letters from headquarters in Cherry Hill, New Jersey, supporting us in our decisions and assuring us of continuing prayer on our behalf. In a practical way, they arranged for credit cards and advanced money to be issued as needed. They promptly relayed information as to our whereabouts to concerned families and friends.

One day when we were returning to the guest house, Bonnie Carlson called to us, "There are more of you arriving today."

Just as she said that, in pulled a taxi carrying the Gurganus family. We all talked at once, eager to share our experiences and learn what had happened since that evening in March when we had last seen them.

Their ship had taken them to Calcutta, where news reporters immediately latched on to the disembarking passengers. Some of the foreigners vocally supported the Bengali cause, but our missionary group had commented, "We refuse to say anything at all in fear for the safety of those left behind."

The Gurganuses explained that the embassies represented by the various nationalities on board had provided hospitality until everyone was able to move on from Calcutta. As soon as possible, the Gurganuses had left for Karachi and on north to join their daughter at the Murree Christian School.

Meanwhile, Vic, Donn, and Reid were back in East Pakistan. Not until much later did we learn what it had meant to be there during those days.

In his personal diary Dr. Donn Ketcham bares his own heart about some of the events of those days. I am indebted to him for allowing me to share a part of it with you.

"April 21, 5:30 A.M. A race up to the hospital to clue in the national staff who knew nothing of our hurried evacuation. It shook them plenty, and they needed multiple reassurances that Vic and I were remaining behind. Back to the house to wind up last-minute business, help load the three cars and trailer, and away we go.

"Jay Walsh (who really wanted to stay behind but was needed to help cope with the travel arrangements) drove a Landrover, as did Joe DeCook and I. We took along a national driver to bring back one of the cars for us. God gave us a cloudy, overcast, rainy day. Besides making the crowded cars more bearable because it was cool, the weather state precluded the possibility of strafing from the air.

"Ordinarily, the border of Burma is closed, but the Burmese are shutting their eyes to the numbers of people coming for refuge. Our government had notified Burma that we were coming, so the way was supposedly prepared. Couldn't help but think of Psalm 105:

> 'When they were but a few men in number; yea, very few, and strangers in it.
> When they went from one nation to another, from one kingdom to another people;
> He suffered no man to do them wrong: yea, he reproved kings for their sakes;
> Saying, Touch not mine anointed, and do my prophets no harm' (vv. 12-15).

"Thank You, Lord.

"Jay made arrangements for the boat. Since the tide was out, we had to wait awhile. But finally the boat was loaded and all the people in. I got there after they were all aboard, since I had been taking care of the currency exchange in the bazaar. Thus I missed the chance for a final kiss from my family. Kit, bless her, was as brave as could be. She never flinched. David and Marty were torn between the pain of leaving Daddy and the excitement of the boat trip across the three-mile-wide river. My Becky cried.

" 'Noah's Ark' pulled slowly out into the stream, and I stood alone on the shore with a heavy heart.

"We had taken three cars, but now with just two drivers going back, I left my car with a national friend. Along the way, the sights that met our eyes! Streams of poor Hindu refugees straggling along the road. Father carrying household goods; pregnant mother carrying another baby and dragging a protesting toddler. Miles from anywhere, all headed south.

"Beautiful cloud formations. *How can the day be so beautiful and the heart so lonely?* I thought. Peaceful countryside . . . who could believe there's a war on? A group of soldiers: grim, determined, but frightened of what lies ahead.

"6 P.M. Arrival back at the hospital. The driveway lined with nationals, their faces beaming to see me back. The last hundred yards of the drive is into the sunset, and the Lord painted an especially lovely one today. I've held up well today, but that sunset did it. I had to stop the car and sob awhile."

Dr. Ketcham had scant time, however, to dwell on what was nearest his heart. Mounting responsibility for the endangered nationals, plus the fact that only he and Dr. Vic Olsen were now charged with the protection of the entire hospital complex, fully occupied his time.

As though to throw these two men more completely upon the Lord, Vic was the victim of a freak motorcycle accident and required surgery.

"A really creamed elbow," Donn Ketcham described it.

Later, Vic wrote to all of us, "I'm sure glad you guys voted for Donn to stay!"

Much water would flow under the bridges of East Pakistan before we, the evacuees, would learn of this accident and other crises at Malumghat and in Chittagong during our enforced exile from the country.

Grateful Bengali survivors still talk about the selfless heroism of the American missionaries. By harboring many Hindus and interceding with the military for the lives of others, Donn Ketcham and Vic Olsen at Malumghat and Reid Minich in Chittagong were responsible, under God, for saving countless lives throughout those days.

Not only were their lives spared, but in numerous instances their material possessions also. Again I draw from Dr. Ketcham's diary:

"May 8th. The day started off peacefully enough, but sort of flew into pieces toward the end. About 4:00 P.M. word came that the military was burning houses in Dulahazara. I hopped on the motorcycle and eased my way into the village to see what was up. The military had left, but not before setting fire to the housing complex of the most powerful Hindu in the village. Several bamboo buildings were just ashes, but the main building was a mud and cement house. It was smoking, but intact. I went to investigate and found about fifty local men looting the place, breaking locks off boxes, etc.

"What to do? On principle I had to do something, so I threw out a bunch bodily and chased out the others, raced back to the hospital, got a car and several of the hospital men, and returned to salvage what I could. I 'preached a little sermon' about kicking a neighbor when he's down. Then I told them I was going to lock the stuff up in the hospital until legal disposition could be made of the goods—and I left. The fellows on the hospital staff, bless them, went into a very dangerous situation without a whimper because I was willing to lead the way."

This was just one of many instances of the incredibile faith the nationals had in Donn and Vic. They brought their valuables to be kept at the hospital, never even requesting a receipt. These people were childlike in their trust of the Americans.

Meanwhile, "American tourists in Thailand," our thoughts were of East Pakistan, the three left there, and how soon we could hope to return.

There goes
Two-a-Penny

8

There goes
Two-a-Penny

Almost as soon as people got the word that we had left East Pakistan, we began getting letters from concerned family and friends. They all sounded alike. "You sure must be glad to be out of *there!* When can we start looking for you to arrive in the States?"

But none of us had any desire to head towards America. We hadn't wanted to leave East Pakistan in the first place, and those of us who had no reentry visa lived in dread of never being able to return. We knew that the Lord had led us out, although we didn't understand what His purpose was in it. All we knew was that we wanted to get back, and the sooner the better. We had left behind in that war-torn land our homes, our possessions, our friends, and our hearts.

While we women enjoyed ourselves shopping and thought up ways to keep the kids entertained, the men were burdened with the problem of getting us out of Bangkok. The complexities of the situation were enormous. Three of the families had teen-agers over in Murree School in West Pakistan. After we had been in Bangkok a few days, we began getting letters from those of our group who had gone to West Pakistan, indicating that some of the kids were frightened and wanted their parents to come. Those who didn't have children there were not pleased at the prospect of spending an exorbitant amount of money to fly to Karachi, only to have to sit and wait it out while official-dom decreed whether we could—or could not—return to the East.

Yet our only hope of ever returning to Pakistan was to stick together as a group who had left the country on the advice of the U.S. government. We reasoned that since they had told us to leave, they would have to see about getting us back in. But it wasn't that easy. There was only so much the Americans could do, and Pakistan was not eager to help us. After all, we had burst their bubble, "Everything is normal in East Pakistan." If everything was so normal, why would the U.S. government make a special point of asking Americans to leave?

To add to the problem, more than half of us had visas which had long since expired. Even in normal times we would have had trouble returning.

In our travels around town, we frequently passed the Pakistan Embassy. Each time we went by, Mel Beals let out a hearty, "Joi Bangla." His wife, Margie, afraid of hostile ears picking this up and holding it against us, asked him to stop saying that.

"All right," he agreed. "I'll keep quiet, but I'm saying it on the inside."

Jay Walsh and Mel Beals commuted back and forth between the American Embassy and the Pakistan Embassy. The Lord was on our side at the latter. The man whose responsibility it would be to issue our permits was from Dacca. Jay, in his relaxed way, started up a conversation with him in Bengali. The official's eyes lit up, and he lowered his voice to ask confidentially what was really happening back in his own country. From then on, he tried his best to help us, but even his best wasn't enough. Final clearance had to come from the Pakistan central government in Islamabad.

Americans visiting in Thailand are only allowed to stay fifteen days. After that they must leave the country and reenter on a new permit. At the end of our fifteen days, we decided we would take a few days' vacation on the island of Penang. As we were boarding the bus to drive out onto the airstrip, an airport operator paged Jay. The message he received was not conducive to our having a happy holiday. The U.S. Embassy had just received a telex from their counterpart in Islamabad, West Pakistan, telling our group that we should not even attempt to enter West Pakistan. U.S. missionaries were being asked to leave from that side too!

There was no one to turn to now but to the Lord. We were reminded of our Assembly of God missionary friend who used to say: "When you feel like there's no place to go but to the Lord, that's like saying there's nothing left to eat but food."

We did turn to the Lord. In private and group prayer the main theme was no longer, "Lord, get us back in," but, "Lord, show us what You want us to do."

The group Jay was traveling with went back to Bangkok a few days before the rest of us. He had scarcely arrived when he was called to the Pakistan Embassy and shown the cable, "Do the needful to allow these people to enter Pakistan."

Jay sized up the situation immediately. He was sure that what Pakistan had in mind was merely a travel permit to allow the parents to pick up their children and leave. However, he caused the official to interpret that cable to mean, "Give them all four-year multiple-entry visas."

Once again God rewarded our little bit of faith by opening His storehouse of good things. Every one of us who needed one —even some whose visas had not yet expired—was given the cream of all visas. That four-year multiple-entry visa meant we could come and go without having to have visas renewed over and over again. Some of our newer missionaries had never had these, having been unable to get them in the States prior to coming to Pakistan.

Jay telephoned the news to the rest of us in Penang, and we gleefully boarded the returning flights to claim our prize. On May 17, Jay took Lynn, Becky, and me to get our visas stamped in our passports. When we stopped at the American Embassy on the way back, the officer of the day said, pointing to Jay, "This man Walsh really shoots for the moon, doesn't he?" Then in a more serious tone, he added, "You've got Somebody up there working for you."

During the weeks while we waited for our visas and tickets, we devoured newspaper reports and rudely peered over the shoulders of anyone reading an article about Pakistan. Accounts like this one, *Newsweek*, 26 April 1971, had special meaning to us.

> . . . In a civil war already marked by brutality, the lightning attacks were notable for their savagery. In the port city of Chittagong, Pakistani troops reportedly forced Bengali prisoners to ride on the front of a truck, shouting, "Victory to Bengal"

— an independence slogan. When other Bengalis emerged from their hiding places, the Pakistanis opened fire with machine guns. . . . In the cities of Sylhet and Comilla, West Pakistani firepower left the bodies of scores of dead peasants to be picked apart by vultures and wild dogs.

We read of refugees pouring into India at the rate of 100,000 a day. We read the tales of human tragedy which those thousands carried with them into the refugee camps: parents murdered in front of their children; infants tossed up into the air and caught on the soldiers' bayonets; young girls dragged off into sexual slavery; men beaten until they lost their eyes.

In spite of these accounts, or perhaps because we thought that maybe we could help, we wanted to return. Yet it was a mighty discouraged group that met together to pray that unbearably hot Bangkok night. We had had our mountaintop experience. God had answered our prayers; we had our visas in hand.

Half of our group had made the decision to go on ahead to West Pakistan with a brief stop in Dacca, the capital of East Pakistan. The thirty-four of us had been together so much in those five weeks since leaving Malumghat Hospital that twelve-year-old Phillip Walsh reluctantly joined his family in the first group, saying, "I really don't think we should break up the group."

Those of us still in Bangkok had rejoiced in hearing that at the brief stop in Dacca, Dr. Olsen had greeted his family, the Walshes, and the Ketchams, and a plan had been worked out whereby they could remain in East Pakistan. They were all back, and here *we* were—still stuck in hot, muggy Bangkok.

The Pakistan Embassy had promised that just as soon as permission came for us to return to Dacca, they would inform us. But days went by and there was no word. Friday, May 29, Mel Beals took up residence at the embassy, but by noon he realized that he might as well give up. In Muslim countries the offices close at noon on Friday, and no government stays open on Saturday and Sunday. There was no possible chance that we could get on the plane leaving on Sunday afternoon.

We had played up the fact that the premier showing of the Billy Graham film "Two-a-Penny" was to be in the Evangelical Church of Bangkok Sunday night, May 31, for the stores, the zoo, and even the swimming pool had lost some of their glamour by this time.

During the prayer time many of us admitted that our faith had hit rock bottom. The others were in; why weren't we? Didn't God want us to go back? Should we go on to the States after sitting it out here all these weeks? Were we supposed to accept our mission board's suggestion that the medical personnel in the group go to assist with the medical program in the Philippines? Lynn didn't say much that night. She had stated her point before; God was going to take us back in—that Sunday!

The Evangelical Church in Bangkok holds its worship service first, followed by a brief intermission, then Sunday school classes. In closing the morning service, the pastor read a message: "If there is a Dr. Cook present, he is wanted on the phone." Our Dr. DeCook figured that was close enough and ran to the nearest telephone. We were already singing the opening hymn in the Sunday school session when he returned, beaming from ear to ear. With a brief explanation to the rest of the congregation, we all filed or, more explicitly, flew out into the lobby.

Poor Joe DeCook could hardly get the story out. Pakistan International Airlines, not wanting to lose such a large number of fares, had put special pressure on the government authorities. The permission to enter was at the PIA office. Could we be ready by 5:00 P.M.? Could we? Half the women were already on the elevator getting ready to leave the hotel in which the Evangelical Church was meeting at the time. I rode up another flight to get the children from their classes and motioned to the junior age group to come quietly and not disturb the rest of the class. They joined me in the hall.

"What's up?" asked ten-year-old Dan.

"We're going home this afternoon, Danny," I answered.

"Home? You mean we're going back to Pakistan? Yippee! I've got to go back in and tell my class. They were just praying that we'd get to go."

The impact of the answered prayer hit us as we rode down those many flights.

"There goes 'Two-a-Penny!'" Dan said as we climbed into the taxi.

What a hustle that afternoon as we hunted for boxes and rope to tie up the extras that we had bought. We didn't know what the food situation would be, so we had stocked up on tinned margarine, meat, and other things. Between the PIA staff and the cordial C. & M.A. guest house personnel, they got us and our overweight baggage out to the airport on time—too early as a matter of fact. The children had plenty of time to get lost in the huge Bangkok waiting room. Going to recover one three-year-old from a barrier over which she was climbing, I overheard an American man asking her where she was going. Little Amy was slightly mixed up after these weeks of traveling.

She answered brightly, "I'm going to Bangkok."

"No, you're in Bangkok. Where are you going now?"

Then he turned to the next little blond, who knew the right answers.

"We're going to Dacca, then to Chittagong," she told him.

"Are you related to these children?" he asked as I stepped up to them.

"We're all traveling together," I explained.

"Oh," he said. "I am pleased to meet you. I'm the American Ambassador to Pakistan."

I have to thank whatever power it was that kept me from saying, "Yes, and *I'm* Mrs. Santa Claus," (or something equally bright) for this ordinary, middle-class type of man didn't at all measure up to my preconceived notions of an ambassador. Then he promptly went into action—like a good politician—shaking everyone's hand, patting the kids' heads, teasing the men about traveling with twice as many women. He left us with a rather disquieting remark:

"I'm surprised that you're going back. Everybody else is trying to get out of there."

And so we stepped onto the plane that was taking us back to the country everybody else wanted to leave. It was midnight before we were able to convince the customs officials that everything was legal and that we had permission to get off in Dacca. The airport personnel were under the impression that no one was allowed to disembark in Dacca.

We settled into the lovely Hotel Inter-Continental, almost too tired to enjoy the hot running water. Surveying the hotel the next day, it resembled a tomb rather than the bustling center of activity that it had become in recent years. Later in the day we were relieved when the remaining missionaries in Dacca came to get us and took us to four separate homes to await permission and tickets to get us to Chittagong.

Dr. Olsen had written a letter and sent it on to await our possible arrival in Dacca. That "Dear Gang" letter filled in the gaps and answered many of the questions that had been plaguing us.

10 May 1971

ABWE Evacuees
Wherever you may be:

Dear Gang:

Greetings from Reid, Donn, and Vic! We are well, and we miss you all, think of you often, and pray for you much. It just doesn't seem right here without you. I am writing from Chittagong—it is the first time I have been here for ages. Reid has given up his apartment and has moved into Gurganus' house which he is able to rent at half price. It is stacked high with Gurganus' stuff and the goods of various and assorted friends who needed to store their goods temporarily. How I have enjoyed these few hours of fellowship with Reid. He is doing a tremendous job moving about the city, encouraging, counseling, and praying with various ones. He has also been able, in a very practical fashion, to help people in many ways.

Following your precipitous departure on April 21, I immediately called our nationals together. Those great verses at the end of Matthew 28, which we considered briefly at the beginning of the meeting, meant a great deal to all of us. We considered the situation and made some tentative decisions. During the most tense part of the meeting, a sudden gigantic, ear-splitting explosion sent everyone scurrying towards windows and doors and diving under the benches—but it was just a freak peal of thunder. I spent the day seeing patients, counseling with the staff members, and increasing the night guard. Other developments later in the day made it prudent to call another meeting at 9:30 P.M. There was some apprehension that there might be active warfare near the hospital. It was decided to evacuate the hospital staff to Hebron and to various villages.

April 22, we were extremely busy implementing the decision of the night before. My accident happened in the morning. While I was riding the motorbike at a good clip, the main member of the frame cracked and the cycle instantly broke into two pieces. When it collapsed, I was thrown into the road, fracturing my right elbow. I made my way to the hospital, arranged my x-ray, read it, and discovered a complicated fracture requiring an operation and insertion of appropriate hardware. As Donn and I had much work to do during the day, we scheduled the operation for 8:00 P.M. Donn did an excellent job. (I'm sure glad you guys voted for him to stay.) The next day was very busy. I laid off the Demerol and was clearheaded by mid-morning and able to move about and make some contribution. Donn worked like a trooper, getting the staff and refugees off the compound.

During the next week we saw a few patients, had a few adventures, and missed you all. The hospital was like a tomb, as we had discharged all the patients. After the departure of the American and Pakistani staff we were considerably threatened by the likelihood of armed robbery. We further increased the night guard and armed them heavily. By God's grace, the night the threats began, the electric power stayed on all night and has continued to do so.

Recently we captured one thief. When the staff departed, it became necessary to move our West Pakistani watchmen to another location for their protection. That night we moved them in with us at the Ketcham house where they stayed until we could hand them over to the military. Their gratitude was something to behold. Although I am not recommending bachelorhood, I have greatly enjoyed this time of fellowship with Donn. He has done a great job as registrar, doctor, nurse, cashier, pharmacist, bookkeeper, etc. He has missed no opportunity to give spiritual help, advice, and comfort as well.

Donn caused a sensation one day when he shot two stray dogs. At the sound of the gun, three nearby villages emptied out. They thought the war had come their way.

We have had five contacts with the government military. On May 5, the advancing army reached the hospital. There was no resistance of any kind. They stopped, and a major and a colonel talked with us for thirty minutes. The sum and substance of these meetings were these points:

—They are happy about the hospital and want it open and operating.

—They guarantee that all hospital staff members, regardless of religion, will be protected and remain safe.

—They requested we call our Pakistani staff back immediately and put them back to work.

Just after our meeting with the military on May 5, a messenger from Hebron brought a letter stating that the folks there were in danger of armed robbery that very night. With the Lord's help it was possible to arrange police protection for that night and for seventeen boats to bring our people from Hebron the following day. Simultaneously we learned that our employees who were staying elsewhere in the jungle also faced a great risk of armed robbery. We immediately sent word to them to come. How wonderful the Lord's timing! Just as intolerable risks and danger arose for our staff, the military came, giving excellent assurance and allowing us to bring them back. The seventeen boats from Hebron contained 120 people, several goats, numerous chickens, and mountains of baggage. It was a tired but elated group of refugees who returned to us on the evening of May 6.

We have made a plan concerning your return. It was not easy to do, since we don't know your visa situation, nor do we know the location of all the evacuees. On May 8, I talked with the Consul General on the phone. He approved the timetable for your return that I outlined to him. According to his statements, his representatives were highly impressed with you all. So, I blushed a little for each of you, thanked him for his kind words, and told him we thought he had sent a pretty fine carload of U.S.A. representatives down our way. By this time, it was getting mushy enough that we decided to get back to business. He offered to send you a message, and no doubt you have received the timetable from him by now.

There are a hundred more points I could mention, but this letter must stop someplace. The three of us testify to the goodness and enabling grace of God. How the Lord has strengthened us at difficult times and given us wisdom for difficult decisions. Today an unusually complex problem with far-reaching implications required action. Our hospital liaison officer and I got into the car and, as the engine was idling, had a word of prayer together — then we were off. And the Lord did work on our behalf beyond our fondest expectation. Our liaison officer said, "What a wonderful thing God did for us. We must not fail to pray again and thank Him for His great works." We are grateful for God's call and your vote that made it possible for us to be here at such a time as this.

God bless you, each one.

Love in Christ,
"Vic"

By the morning of June 3, all was in order, and we climbed onto the last plane — a forty-minute ride to Chittagong. We had tried to telephone; the lines were out of order. We had sent a cable; the telegram never arrived. Consequently, there was no one to meet us at the airport. Fortunately PIA allowed us to make use of their bus, and the driver took us to our mission guest house. The outside gate was chained and padlocked, so he drove us on to our office. The watchman there said that Reid Minich who had the keys to everywhere had left that morning to go to the hospital — sixty-five miles of bad road away. The bus driver was getting tired of playing Good Samaritan and announced that he would take us to the PIA downtown terminal, and there we had to get off. That was fine. The terminal was just a minute or so away from our apartment. Climbing into the three-wheeled, motorized baby-taxis, we rode around to our house. I was so excited at being back among the Bengali people again, that seeing an old lady on our verandah, I just hugged her. Later I began to wonder who she was and what she was doing there.

It was noon by this time, and everybody was hungry. Reid had the keys to our house too, but tucked away in my purse was one key that opened up the pantry where we kept canned food. Bread was available from around the corner. With tinned sandwich meat, soup packets, and hot cokes, also from around the corner, everybody got something to eat. The men had rounded up a bus to take the hospital people down to Malumghat. By 2:00 P.M. the "group" had broken up for good.

Lynn and I sat on the floor in the living room trying to realize that we were back. We didn't have the keys to get into our own rooms, but we weren't alone in the house. Jabbor's wife and the two little boys had preceded us back by a few days. They had gone with us when we evacuated to the hospital and had fled from there up the river to our jungle station, only to be returned to the hospital when the threat of robbery broke out. Now they were back in our house. The old lady on the verandah was a relative of some kind staying in the house until Jabbor himself returned from checking on the condition of his parents and village home.

Bengalis. Our people. We were *home.*

But it was not yet the land of "Joi Bangla!"

Reunion and rumblings

9

Reunion and rumblings

"Well, it's about time you two were here! I've come around so many times these past few months and you girls are never home."

Reid — returned from Malumghat with our keys in hand.

We pumped him for all the news of our friends and church people. He answered our endless questions and told us some of his experiences.

On one trip when he was carrying medicines and supplies to our hospital, Reid followed on the heels of a military platoon. As he pulled into the town of Patiya, the soldiers were setting fire to the shops lining the road. A major motioned Reid to stop directly opposite the white-hot conflagration. Seeing the fierceness of the blaze and feeling its intense heat, he was afraid of an explosion in the car's gas tank or in the burning shops, so he drove a little farther down the road out of the direct line of the fire.

The officer charged after him screaming, "When I tell you to stop, you stop! Wherever I am, it is safe."

Many months passed before Reid disclosed the following incident.

"The harassment in Chittagong was increasing. I recall the evening when I had just heard the martial law announcement that the curfew hours had been changed from 8:00 to 9:00 P.M., effective immediately. At 7:30, one of our teenage boys came and said, 'They have just taken my father away.'

"If I had not heard the announcement of the curfew change," Reid explained, "I might not have been able to do anything that night.

"I went to the municipal office. The guard was not co-operative. The boy's father had given a different name so as not to be thought a Hindu (the crime of all crimes). Five soldiers walked up. They would not admit that the man was in custody or permit me to see him. 'This man must not be beaten. He is a *Christian*,' I insisted, then left to come back in the morning."

(In many cases, "Christian" spelled immunity. Perhaps because the West Pakistani soldiers equated "Christian" with America or perhaps because God wanted to show the world that He really does care for His own in a special way, Christians often were spared the torture and indignities.)

"In the morning I took John Sircar (our fine national literature worker) to the arrested man's house. I had to know if this father was innocent of Awami League activities; if he was not politically involved, then the military had no case for holding him. From his family and all his neighbors I got signed statements to this effect. (I learned this procedure from the local Catholic priest who had tried it.) With this assurance that the man was being held improperly, I prepared a summary statement in his defense and returned to the Municipal Office. At first they wouldn't admit me. Then I located a higher police official who confirmed that the man was there. I went upstairs and found him crouched on the floor. His hands were tied behind him; he had been badly beaten. There was blood on his shirt. I could not stand idly by.

"I picked up the minister of the Anglican Christ Church, Rev. David Davey, and together we went to Major Bhukari at the military headquarters, the Circuit House. The guards at the door did not stop us, so we walked directly up to the major's desk.

"The major snarled, 'You should have waited until the guards let you in.' He then began tearing into David, so I spoke up. 'One of our Christian men has been taken,' I explained, showing him the statement that I had prepared. At that he hit the ceiling. His face livid, he screamed, 'What you have done is *against the State of Pakistan!* Only our military can investigate a case. You are under arrest!'

"'Can I call my consulate?' I inquired.

"'Certainly not! Sit down!'

"It was obvious that both David and I were under arrest. The major continued his tirade: 'Why don't you help the Urdu-speaking people?' — and he gave us a crocodile tears' tale of a widow whose husband had been shot.

"By now I was thinking, *I have the Gurganus' VW and all their furniture and the responsibility of the girls' house and all the property at our office. What if I'm given twenty-four hours to get out of the country? What if I don't get out?* I knew then what it really means to pray for deliverance. Only the Lord could handle this.

"We were taken outside under guard and made to sit under a tree and wait. After some time the irate major returned. He had gone to the Brigadier.

"'You can go,' Major Bhukari spat out the reprieve, 'but we don't ever want to see you here again. We are letting you go because we do not want to create an international incident.'

"I praised God for His deliverance all the more because there are numerous instances of people being shot, not officially, but because of some enraged individual. I realized that this major would have loved to have issued the command, 'Shoot him.' The goodness of God and the fact that I was an American saved my life.

"I went to the imprisoned man's house to tell the family that I would not be able to do any more for him. Suddenly, with no explanations, he was released. And they had *not* beaten him again after my first visit.

"'You're fortunate,' they told him. 'A foreign sahib came looking for you.'"

On that first day back in Chittagong, Reid advised us to lay low, and not make it conspicuous that we were back. People were used to seeing him around, and it gave many of them courage to know that there were still some foreigners in town. In fact, Reid made a point of wearing the same shirt — a gold-colored one — every time he went out so that he would be recognized easily. We began to call it his "brave shirt."

For the first few days after our return, we couldn't have gone anywhere. It took us that long to scrub out the dirt, the blood stains, and the mess that we had left behind in March.

When we began to visit our friends, we had a baby-taxi come right up to the door. We climbed in quickly, went where we were going, stayed a short time, and got right back to our house. We never stood out on the streets, and we did little shopping. We never went out after sundown by ourselves.

Even in the cautious selected outings that we made, we could feel the difference in the atmosphere around us. Everywhere you turned there were troops marching the streets with their guns ready; glaring down at you from the back of an open truck; barging their way into shops to help themselves to what they wanted. This was not two halves of the same country trying to reconcile internal differences. This was the occupation of a defenseless country by a stronger power.

Fear was written on every face. Mothers hushed their tiny tots' singing in case they would break into the once popular "Joi Bangla" chant. Gone were the ever-present groups who loitered on the roadsides half the night. Scarcely a sound or movement was heard after dark. Once when driving home from a rare evening out Reid encountered a band of wild jackals running down the main street of the city at 9:30 in the evening.

Even in the daytime things were quiet. Once I had complained that I "lived in a supermarket," because without ever moving off my verandah I could have bought shoes, bedcovers, live fish, pots and pans, fresh fruits and vegetables, sets of dishes, eggs, a complete change of clothes, doormats, brooms, ice cream, candy, hot meat patties, patent medicine. I could have had my scissors sharpened or my shoes repaired. I could have sold used paper and bottles. Now even the hawkers had abandoned the streets.

A door slamming in the wind, a tire bursting, a car backfiring: these noises sent the usually indolent people scaling the nearest wall or running for cover. All too often the noises were real — the crack and whine of bullets.

We *had* to go shopping sometimes. In the center of Chittagong stands a four-story collection of shops known as New Market. At 6:30 one evening we were shopping in a cloth store. Suddenly people rushed past us on all sides.

"The military are coming! The military are coming!" The cry rang out through the cement structure. Quickly the old proprietor pulled us inside and slammed down the overhead sliding metal door.

"Don't be afraid. Don't be afraid," he kept saying over and over, though whether he was speaking to us or to himself, we didn't know. The shots came, but not from inside the building. It had been a false alarm that time. The railway station, a quarter of a mile away, was under attack.

Lynn and I wanted to see all our friends and hear about their experiences. Carefully we went from house to house, listening, sharing, praying, and rejoicing in the ways that God had spared them. One of the first rounds of visits was to the homes of the teenage girls in my Sunday school class. God had planned our timing perfectly. As soon as we entered the first house, we saw that the mother of one of the girls was dangerously ill. Checking her blood pressure and physical symptoms, we recognized the warning signs of a toxic pregnancy. She needed to be hospitalized immediately. Each of her seven daughters had been born at home, so the family would never have considered taking her to a hospital, nor would they have been able to had they realized the necessity. Quickly we made the arrangements and settled her in the British Baptist Hospital at Chandraghona.

On the way to the hospital, the mother confided in us that she was mortally afraid for the safety of her oldest daughter during these troubled times. We assured her that God was able to take care of her girls. Then God took us up on that and reminded us that He has chosen to work through human instruments to accomplish His will. Shortly after the mother returned from Chandraghona with a beautiful baby boy, sixteen-year-old Lucy came to live with us.

Another afternoon as we were sitting on the bed in a one-room house that faced the street, we suddenly looked up to see two uniformed men enter. One was quite loquacious, asking ridiculous questions as he leered at us.

"What are you?"

"Are you Bengali?"

"Are you white?"

His partner seemed eager to end the dialogue and move on, but the spokesman continued, "What do you do?"

Seeing that we were getting nowhere with our explanations, an old lady began speaking to him in Urdu. "This is a Christian village. These ladies have come here to pray with us."

"Oh," he answered as the light broke through. "You are goddesses!"

As missionaries in chaotic Chittagong we were daily conscious of the presence and leading of the Lord; but we were also aware that our Father was showing Himself strong on behalf of individual national believers.

Here an Anglo-Indian man and his wife relate their experiences of deliverance that can be explained only by the supernatural. These are the *true experiences* of Mr. Jimmy Rodgers and his wife, written in their own words.

"Had Mr. Zulfiqar Ali Bhutto not torpedoed the convening of the National Assembly of Pakistan on 3 March 1971, I would not have a story to tell.

"Orphaned at the age of six, I entered into the great orphanage founded by the late Dr. J. A. Graham, nestling in the foothills of the Himalayas. Our whole lives were overshadowed by the ever-changing face of majestic Mt. Kanchenjunga. The orphanage was a Christian institution where I not only received a fine education, but received Christ as my Savior and began a habit of Bible reading and prayer.

"Unfortunately, I forgot those early experiences when I entered the Navy during World War II. Wars can either draw one closer to God or nearer to Satan, depending on the depth of faith and the company one keeps. My falling away from the faith was a slow process: first drinking and card playing, then farther and farther away from Christ until apart from murder, in the eyes of the law, there wasn't a sin that I hadn't committed.

"Finally coming to the end of myself and finding myself in a position of being falsely accused of robbery, I called out to God. One minute my life was in darkness and deep depression; the next minute all was light, strength, and assurance. Many years passed — years of regular employment, climbing steadily in my field. Since we had no children of our own, my wife and I adopted two little Bengali girls.

"We were comfortable and reasonably well off. Then the sky fell on us. I lost my job and had to work at various things for short periods during the next six months. In March 1971 I was working in Dacca. My wife and two little girls, then three and four years old, were in Chittagong, 175 miles to the south.

Our house was situated about a half a mile from a predominantly Bihari area and adjacent to a paramilitary camp. It was in a lonely spot with only one other house nearby.

"On December 27, when I was home for Christmas, I had a strong premonition that I would not see my house again. This feeling persisted so strongly that I wrote a missionary friend, Gene Gurganus, in Chittagong, outlining my fears and asking him to look after my family.

"On March 1, Sheikh Mujibur Rahman gave a clarion call to all Bengalis to resist the disruptive activities of our erstwhile western wing brothers who were putting many obstacles in the way of convening the National Assembly. The whole of the east wing rose to his call. From March 1 to March 25, the situation was tense and riots took place. On 25 March, 1971 the Pakistani military forces started an all-out action to subdue the Bengalis, and in the main they succeeded.

"Although Dacca was subdued overnight, the fighting in Chittagong continued for twenty days. On March 25 at about 10:00 P.M., the guns and rifles boomed and sputtered in Dacca. I could not sleep. At 2:00 A.M., the military were going around the town and warning everyone through loudspeakers that a curfew had been called for the entire day (March 26). Anyone leaving his house would be shot to death.

"By that afternoon I couldn't bear the pangs of hunger any longer, so braving the curfew I stealthily left my house and started looking for food. I found a small thatched house with a small opening where tea was being sold. I filled up a quart bottle with it, as that was all the food I could find on my forage. The next day I managed a stale loaf of bread and more tea from this same small shop. Four Bengali families had moved in with me for refuge. As I was living in a single room, 10x10 feet, you can imagine the difficulties involved.

"On March 28 I tried to get back to my family in Chittagong. Twice I went to the cantonment to get an air permit but was effectively brushed off. On April 3 I got a friend who spoke Urdu to try to arrange the permit for me. He managed to do so, but put himself in terrible trouble. Then he asked me to accompany him to the military officer who was issuing air permits. Upon my arrival, I was told that my friend was using my name to get a ticket for himself. They had every intention of shooting him, but I managed to extricate my friend from his predicament. He told me that he had been lined up to be shot but had pleaded his innocence. Since he was able to speak Urdu, the language of the West Pakistanis, he was given the chance to get me to come and substantiate his story. Of course I did not get my air permit that day. Throughout the rest of the week I lined up for a permit but was refused because I had no proof that I was a Pakistani. After five futile attempts, the permit was granted for a flight on May 6.

"The night before my scheduled flight, I received a telegram stating that my wife and children were safe and currently living in the Bible Information Center. This gave me quite a shock. I knew immediately that something had happened to our house, otherwise my wife never would have left home. But how can I explain the timing of that telegram? Had I received my air permit any earlier, I would have gone straight to my house; seeing its condition, I would have assumed that my wife and children had been killed. Receiving the telegram when I did spared me heartache and panic. Having received this news, I went straight to the Bible Information Center and was re-united with my family. As the days went by, I learned my wife's side of the story. I will let her tell it."

"Riots broke out near our house on March 3, but quite quickly everything was under control outwardly. March 25 was a normal sort of day. In the evening I had gone to my neighbors, a family with eighteen members. I asked if they had any intention of leaving, but they led me to understand that we were safe in this isolated area. I returned home, had a quiet night's sleep, and woke up the next morning with no worry of what was to follow.

"At ten o'clock, in the morning, a man from the nearby para-military came and asked me to check on the condition of my neighbors as there were no sounds of movement from the house. I went and found it empty and locked from the outside. I was annoyed and dismayed that they could be so mean; after giving me full assurance that we were safe, they had slipped away without letting me know they were going! I regretted my hasty thoughts about this family when I learned later that all eighteen members had been killed that night.

"On March 27 I had fed the children and done all my house-hold chores when the washerman came. I had no news about the outside world, so I pestered him with questions. He told me that fierce fighting was going on in the city which was about two miles from our house. We were still talking when shells fired from a navy ship started falling around us, covering the area with a heavy mist of dust.

"My husband had often told me about his experiences in the Second World War. He had mentioned that the safest place to take cover was under a table or a bed. We decided that this was the time to try that tactic, so all of us, including the washerman, crawled under the bed. Hardly had we done so when a rocket hit the roof and burst through into the room where we were. The bed broke over our heads. The washerman was injured by shrapnel in his leg and thigh. Shrapnel bit holes into our fridge thirty-two feet away. Terrified, we got out from under the bed and fled in panic, leaving the house wide-open. We ran toward the place from which the shells were coming, dropping to the ground each time a shell whined over-head. Looking back on the scene, the situation seems comic, for we were bobbing up and down into the mud and slush with no concern for how we looked.

"We continued traveling in this manner until we reached the Hindu village. The Hindus begged us to leave their hamlet as they were afraid of reprisals against them. We rested for a while, after which the washerman took us to his village. He then decided to return to the military camp to have his wounds treated. I begged him not to go, but in spite of my entreaties he went — went to his death.

"Before dawn the next day the men in the washerman's village asked me to leave; the fighting was getting very close, and my being in the village might endanger them more. Once again I moved on with our two little girls. About three hundred yards down the road I saw a crowd of grim-looking men armed with swords, knives, and daggers. Finding no other alternative, and with a prayer on my lips, I walked straight towards them. One man asked me if I was the wife of such and such a person, describing my husband perfectly. When I assured him that I was, he told the rest of his band I was under his protection and they should not harm me. Then he personally escorted me to the Chittagong port area where he took me to a Roman Catho-lic Christian's house. This man asked me my name.

"'Rajkumari,' I replied.

"'That's not a Christian name,' he answered. 'That's a Hindu name. I cannot give you shelter.'

"I told my protector and guide that I had a Muslim friend in this area but I didn't know his exact address. After some inquiries, we located this man. He took us in, gave us food, let us wash off the dirt of the trip, and even gave his own children's dresses to my two little girls, as their clothes were in rags. While we were resting, he made inquiries and learned that the military had complete control of the area where our house was. He pleaded with me to return there before everything in the house was stolen. With trepidation I started back with the children, but with the very conscious presence of Jesus at my side.

"On my way back I saw that the washerman's village and the Hindu village where we first had stopped had been completely destroyed. Seeing this, instead of going directly home, I circled to another area where I had some friends. Five of them accompanied me to my house. Besides the direct hit on the roof, there were hundreds of bullet holes in all the walls, both inside and outside, evidence that a running battle had been fought in those very rooms. Most of the windowpanes were broken. My radio, money, and jewelry were gone. We took away as much as my friend's jeep would hold. My helpers wished to go back for a second load, but I was too tired and only wanted to sleep. We did return the next day, but the looters had gotten there first. Unable to break through the securely locked doors, they had broken a portion of the iron grill work at the windows and removed everything that could pass through the window.

"During that week, Reid Minich of the Association of Baptists came looking for me. He obtained official permission to enter the locked house and, fighting against a 5:00 P.M. curfew, removed as many loads of furniture as was possible within the time limit. Then he took us to live in the Bible Information Center where we would be with other Christian friends. My husband returned from Dacca and rejoined us on May 6. He can continue our story."

"When I rejoined my family, it appeared to me that my wife was still getting over the shock of what she had experienced. I had only six days' leave from my job and then had to return to Dacca. Upon my return there, I was told that I no longer fit in with their organization and my services were no longer required. I flew back to Chittagong—jobless, penniless, and homeless.

"We lived at the center for a few months until I found a job in the jute mill, which enabled us to move into a rented house. I thought the clouds were breaking and sunlight would come into our lives. But this was not to be.

"On December 17 the Pakistan army surrendered, and we rejoiced with our Bengali friends. The following day while returning home from visiting friends, the wheel of the rickshaw broke under us, and all were slightly injured. On Demember 23 a car hit the rickshaw in which my wife and children were riding. My wife was seriously injured, and one little girl received head and facial injuries. Our house became a small hospital while I cared for them all.

"Then on Christmas day I became ill. When I began coughing blood, I had to be hospitalized, but the doctor diagnosed my condition as treatable pneumonia, not T.B. as I had feared. This illness prevented me from reporting to work on the appointed day. When I was able to report, I was told that they did not need me; for the second time I was jobless.

"Earlier in December I visited our home, intending to begin necessary repairs. But what a sight confronted me! The house had been completely stripped and left in a shambles. Only the bare walls remained. All the furniture, to the smallest piece of wood, had been taken. Even the doors with the lintels and the posts, the bathroom fixtures, and the electric wiring had been removed.

"But despite our present circumstances, we could see God's good hand upon us. I had felt the premonition of impending danger, yet God took me away from my family. Had I stayed, I would never have left the house. And since the battle went right through the house, we would all have been killed.

"Our only neighbors were killed. Perhaps because my wife was alone she was spared, but the prime question is, 'Who was in control of this situation?'

"Who prompted my wife to take shelter under the beds at just the right time?

"Who caused her to run out of the house against all common sense?

"Who prompted her to run in the direction *from which the shells were coming?* Had she taken the only other and the more natural course, she would have run right into the hand-to-hand fighting in the Bihari colony.

"Who caused the washerman and the Hindu villagers to ask her to leave?

"Who placed men and women with kind hearts right where they could help?

"Yes, God is in complete and firm control! How glorious to know that one is a child of His!"

Such stories inspired us and encouraged us to reach out by every means possible. How much our Bengali people were to need the strength that comes from God alone. The dogs of war were being unleashed again.

Bombed ship in Chittagong port

A mass grave — grisly reminder of war

Trucks outside the rest house in Maungdaw

Weary travelers (from left): Joan Olsen, Joyce and
Joe DeCook, Jeannie, Lynn

Wall-to-wall missionaries

Mrs. Boshu and Jeannie
prepare to leave
on relief mission

Khoka Sen preaches the Gospel
as people gather for relief goods

The victims of war

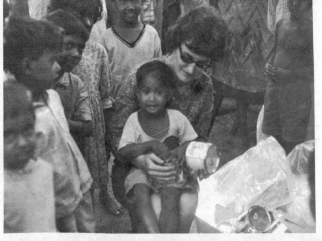

The Nundy sisters whose hideout was their roof

Mrs. Shushama Akand (l) and Lucy (r)

Jeannie's nine girls at "Safe Haven"

Our Mukti Bahini

10

Our Mukti Bahini

Christians and Muslims were caught in the backlash of the military fury, but the crack of the whip was aimed at the Hindus. The Pakistan government blamed the 10,000,000 Hindus in the East for being the chief supporters of Sheikh Mujibur Rahman. The Hindus did, in fact, support Mujib, but so must have some 60,000,000 of other faiths in order for him to have won such an overwhelming victory. The *Weekly Economist* (London) 29 May 1971, in describing the flood of Hindus who fled across to India, reported:

> The migration of the Hindus is a classic case of how propaganda can become self-fulfilling. Just after the March action, West Pakistani newspapers began accusing the Hindus in East Bengal of having illicit links with the Indians. The army then made the Hindus a special target for revenge, forcing them to flee to India in disproportionate numbers. This is now taken as proof that the Hindus were Indian saboteurs all along.

Every Hindu was suspected of pro-India, anti-Pakistan activity. We could watch from our house as columns of Hindu men were marched down the road with their hands tied behind their backs. Many of them never returned.

It was this discrimination that brought the Nundy family to us. During the first week after our return, a man came to our door. He looked familiar, but it was not until a number of visits later that I remembered he was the man who had come for sleeping medicine for his wife in March when we were treating the freedom fighters.

"Can you give me a certificate stating that I am a Christian?" he asked.

We explained that this was not something that could be done on the spur of the moment and set up an appointment for him to meet with Reid Minich. Week after week the two men sat in our living room discussing the things of the Lord.

Bit by bit Mr. Nundy's story came out. He had been standing on the corner of our street the day that the Landrover with the fourteen of us in it pulled away. He had asked one of the children in the car where we were going.

"To our hospital," she replied.

From that day on, whenever anyone asked where his teenage daughters were, he protected them by saying that they had gone to "our hospital."

"By the way," he asked, months later, "where is that hospital?"

Mr. Nundy had been a prominent Hindu businessman. When the trouble began, he had a court action taken giving him a Muslim name, but he was afraid that he would be forced to give his daughters in marriage to a Muslim family; rather than do that, he would become a Christian.

Nine times the military or Bengali collaborators came to the Nundy house asking questions, probing and searching. "Where are you hiding the freedom fighters?" "Where are your arms and ammunition?" "Let us see your whole family."

At the first sound of footsteps, the three beautiful daughters, thirteen, fifteen and eighteen, raced to the back of the house. Shinnying up the side of a wall, they got a toehold on the top of the bathroom door and swung themselves up onto the slanting roof. Scratched and bruised, they clung to the edge of the roof until it was safe for them to return. Meanwhile, inside, the soldiers tried to get the little brothers and sisters to tell them where the girls were.

The military disconnected the telephone, which effectively put an end to Mr. Nundy's insurance business. They killed the Nundy's well-trained Alsatian dog in order to be able to enter the house with less interference. Then back they came. Once the eight-year-old boy opened the door, greeted the men, and shook hands in a respectful manner as he had been taught to do.

Then realizing what was happening, he pleaded with them, "Don't take my daddy away."

But they did take him away. With his hands tied behind his back and walking barefooted, Mr. Nundy had to march two miles to the Circuit House. En route he was mocked, kicked, and slapped. Inside the Circuit House grounds, he and the other prisoners were led to an open field. There he watched others being whipped and tortured.

Stepping up to the officer, he declared, "Why should I be insulted like this? Here is a rupee and ten paise—the cost of a bullet. Go ahead and shoot me!"

Taken aback by his boldness, the military released him.

"Where are my neighbors who were brought here with me?" he questioned, adding, "What does the holy Koran say about loving your neighbors?" They let them all go that day.

Later the military changed their tactics towards this man whom they could not break and offered to pay him fifty rupees every time he informed them of a Bengali rebel attack. Foolishly they approached him while he was standing in the middle of an open-air food bazaar and whispered their proposal to him. Mr. Nundy pretended not to understand what they were saying and made them repeat it over and over again, louder and louder each time.

Finally, in exasperation they screamed at him, "Are you deaf?" and walked away.

Week after week he came to our house to listen to the simplicity of the Gospel story. He read both the Bengali Bible and simplified editions of the English. He and his daughters studied the Bible Correspondence School courses. As often as it seemed wise, we slipped across to the next street and quietly talked with the girls and their mother. The girls are talented musically: they sing beautifully and play the organlike harmonium, the guitar and other stringed instruments, but there could be no singing in those days—nothing to reveal the girls' presence.

Poor people suffered terribly as food prices rose and commodities became scarce, but for many of them this trouble meant tightening belts that were used to being tightened from time to time. For those who belonged to a higher class of society, however, the loss of necessities and luxuries that they had become used to was harder to take. We tried to help them materially, supplying them with some of the relief goods. Mrs. Nundy, being an excellent seamstress, was able to get involved in the remaking of the clothes that we gave to really poor people.

One night in September when I was clearing away the tea cups, Mr. Nundy looked up and said, "Now I could have that certificate. I've found out what it means to become a Christian."

That decision didn't stop the military from their "routine search for miscreants." Early one evening four men appeared at their door: two were masked Bengali informers and the other two were uniformed soldiers. Eight-year-old Prodip dashed around to the side of the house and unchained the two yapping dogs. (We had been able to give them a pair of dachshunds left by foreigners.) The dogs jumped up on the masked men and scared them so that they vaulted back over the fence and ran, but the military men proceeded into the house. By this time, Prodip had returned. Stalking up to the long-since dead telephone, he lifted the receiver, dialed, and began to carry on a conversation.

"Who are you calling?" the soldiers asked.

"Our American friend, Mr. Minich," Prodip answered.

"Oh, well," the men fumbled, "there has been some kind of a mistake here." And with profuse apologies for disturbing the family, the soldiers left.

The brave little boy had saved his father from further humiliation—and even possible death.

Among the indignities to which the Hindus were subjected by the West Pakistani Army was that of a man being commanded to spit on the ground. When he had complied, he was then ordered to "Get down and lick it up." The demand was accompanied with the dig of a rifle butt.

The culture of the country calls for jewels in the women's ears and noses and in bracelets and necklaces, often comprising the family's total wealth. During those months the soldiers would rudely snatch the jewels without regard to how they did it. They also took currency from the banks, stock from the stores, and commandeered private cars and had them driven aboard their ships in the harbor of Chittagong and taken off to West Pakistan.

And all the while they hunted Hindus.

The Nundys were not the only ones who came to us asking for "a paper to say I am a Christian." We encountered many such requests. Actually these pleas gave us wonderful opportunities to explain that a person doesn't become a Christian by signing a paper or a membership roll, or even by baptism or church membership; that real Christianity involves an act of faith whereby the person admits he is unable to save himself and accepts God's gift of salvation. Some listened; others were in too much of a hurry to get that precious piece of paper in their hands.

Certificates were necessary for every phase of life. Anyone who was moving about had to carry an identification card with a picture, a physical description, and place of employment written on it. We found ourselves writing many letters to help people get from one place to another. If they were carrying any equipment or relief goods or even their own personal possessions, we added this clause to the letter: "and if later (certain articles) are not in his hands, we will regard this as a most serious matter." We didn't know what, if anything, we could do to enforce action regarding this "serious matter," but it said to the officials, "Someone is concerned over this person and will take steps to see he is treated fairly."

Soon it became evident that many of the guards at the checkpoints couldn't read the certificates and official letters. People were passing through on food ration cards and student-rate passes. One American presented an expired Marine Midland Bankcard and passed through.

Naturally the guards at the checkposts were on the lookout for Hindus. Many people saved their lives by saying, "I am a *barber,*" or a *washerman,* or a *cobbler,* or a *fisherman.* The West Pakistani did not realize that these designations were part of the caste system of the Hindu religion which thus segregates people into various categories.

Traveling to anywhere became a major nuisance. Bags had to be opened and inspected. At the airport every man was frisked. Women were either Geiger-countered or discreetly examined in a little curtained-off room. It took longer to examine the sari-clad women than it did the westerners because a woman could easily conceal a small armory within the folds of her six yards of cloth. No hand luggage could be carried on board. Once aboard, there was no longer any "Welcome. We hope you enjoy your trip"—not even a cup of tea. Rather, an armed officer speaking first in Urdu, then in English—remember,

Bengali is the language of East Pakistan—announced that you were not to move out of your seat during the flight.

For a while everyone was required to fly the Pakistani flag as a display of their loyalty to the government. The green and white star and crescent appeared on schools, shops, cars, and even on pocket-size flags pinned to men's shirts and ladies' saris. Forced to tear down their own flag, the Bengalis' very souls chafed against having to wear this symbol. Our car repairman made this clear.

Pointing to the Pakistani flag on his pocket, he said, "Please excuse this. It's only on the outside. Another flag is in the heart."

Reading the censored newspaper was a farce. Bold print declared that the whole Bangladesh freedom movement was a stunt. It was purported to be the idea of a few "miscreants" or "Indian infiltrators." If all that was going on was the work of a few miscreants, they certainly were busy. Electric transformers were blown up, cutting the power supply and thus crippling any industry which could bring in revenue for the Pakistan government. Pumps at gas stations were destroyed so that military vehicles would be stopped. Hand grenades, land mines, and homemade bombs all "happened" to explode in strategic places. Bridges were blown up to inhibit troop transport. These things were daily occurrences, yet people who were loyal to Pakistan, whether by conviction or convenience, continued to suggest their proposals for peace:

— Make Urdu the national language. (All signs had been repainted at the beginning of the military occupation because signs in English or Bengali made it impossible for the Urdu-speaking people to tell where they were.)

— All members of the Awami League Working Committee, persons who fired at any army personnel, students who burned the Pakistani flag or pictures of Jinnah, "The Father of the Nation," were to be killed.

— Any of the staff of Radio Pakistan who sang the "Victory to Bengal" song or in any way supported the freedom movement were to be punished.

— Religious instruction was to be given in the schools and colleges to promote the concept of one Pakistan.

— No Bengali was to be recruited for the army or police force.

— All West Pakistani businessmen were to be given gun and ammunition licenses free of charge (otherwise they would leave East Pakistan and the strength of the pro-Pakistan faction and commercial activity would decrease).

Was it any wonder that the hatred between the Bengalis and West Pakistanis flourished? The feeling was strong among nearly all levels of society, but, of course, the freedom fighters were best supported by the eager young people. Some students refused to attend school or college in protest against the government. In many cases the schools were closed anyway; some of the best teachers had been Hindus. They had been killed or were now in hiding. Students and other young men furnished most of the manpower for the Mukti Bahini, the Bengali freedom fighters. We began to suspect that some of the young people in our church were involved when boys who normally were faithful in attending services were suddenly absent. Mrs. Dass's nephew, Stephen, who worked part-time in the literature department, would suddenly have an important appointment for which he could not be late.

Stephen stayed on in the Dass's house after they fled from the city. Next door lived Babla and his family. Babla's mother fed the Mukti Bahini boys who slept next door. When freedom was a reality, Babla shared with us something of his part in the struggle for liberation.

"I saw my chance to witness to my faith in Christ as the Mukti Bahini came to our house," Babla told us. "I always thanked God for the food as they sat at our table. Gradually they began to trust me a little. They first asked me to distribute leaflets with their two-fold message: to encourage our people that victory and freedom were possible, and to urge them to noncooperation with the military.

"They gave me training in guerrilla fighting," he told us and showed the handwritten training manual that someone trained in India had memorized and then produced in handwriting for the others. About two thousand young men from Chittagong had gone for training. Some who went as refugees trained with the freedom fighters, then returned to carry out their assignments of "hit and run without sacrificing your own life."

We learned that we too had been part of the intrigue—at least Lynn's tape recorder had. On the pretext of its keeping Stephen from feeling too lonely in the house "all alone," the boys had borrowed the tape recorder. In the daytime Stephen recorded Urdu music from Radio Pakistan; in the evening they played the tape loudly while the Mukti Bahini group held their strategy meetings in the bedroom.

The patrolling military never suspected their presence, though one day someone did come just to sit down and talk. In case he was really out to get information, Babla was assigned to follow him and make reports so that the Mukti Bahini could abduct him.

Describing some of his specific acts of sabotage, Babla explained, "We *had to* destroy in order to handicap the military."

It was so out of character for this boy I had known for a number of years. He had attended Sunday school and had made his commitment to Christ at one of our camps. He came to church during the entire time that he was in the Mukti Bahini.

"As a Christian, how did you feel about what you were doing?" we asked him. "What made you join the Mukti Bahini?"

"At first," he said, "it was the sheer adventure of it." His dark eyes were merry, but as he continued, his face grew solemn. "But then it was a chance to do something for my country. It was love for my country that made me do the things I did.

"Before joining, I went to Mr. Minich and consulted with him. He showed me in the Bible—from Romans—that I must be loyal to my country. Then I said to him, 'Mr. Minich, you have what you call the draft in America. If you were drafted for your country's service, would you go?' He said, 'Yes, I would go.'"

That was Babla's mandate as a Christian—to join the freedom fighters. He was assigned to intelligence work and was trained from "stand at ease to bazooka shelling," he told us. Because he and Stephen "were not very good at tossing hand grenades, we practiced as though we were throwing a cricket ball"—right under the nose of the military.

One of the schemes the freedom fighters had for outwitting the military was letting it be assumed that the Mukti Bahini had their own transportation, when in fact they rode the commonly used public vehicle, the baby-taxi that shoots all over the place ducking between people, goats, cows, buses, and trucks. Two freedom fighters would travel together. They would give involved directions to the driver; then when confused, he would have to stop and get his bearings. One boy would keep him occupied while the other tossed out the morale-building leaflets —and sometimes a hand grenade. Other common people were used in the fight too: beggars carried ammunition in their begging bowls; oxcart drivers hid arms among the bales of jute or cotton; farmers kept their guns beside the furrow they were plowing.

More hazardous was the blowing up of transformers, As Babla described his part in such missions, again he grew emotional about having to destroy in order to realize their goal.

"Better to destroy some things than to wait another twenty-five years (since the partition of India)for our freedom. We would rebuild, we knew, and the world would help us."

He never started the day without his own quiet time with the Lord, and when Babla was out on a mission, his mother never slept. She proudly watched her handsome son go off, then prayed for him and his compatriots. This brave Bengali woman did her part too. The sector commander of the Mukti Bahini slept in Babla's bed each night, and Babla's mother risked much by feeding him and the others who mysteriously came and went from next door. Besides feeding and praying, she had other tasks. When a Mukti Bahini member appeared at the door, she dispensed weapons and ammunition. Later Babla took us into his bedroom and in guarded secrecy showed us his SMG—submachine gun—and his Colt .38 handgun.

The chief danger to the boys lay in the fact that directly behind their houses was a Razakar camp. The Razakars were a group of hoodlums hired by the government and raised to paramilitary status. They were turncoat Bengalis, informers, who by their Gestapo-like tactics terrorized the people.

The day came when Babla's mother's heart quaked. With three others, Babla left on their most dangerous mission of all: the blowing up of an important bridge, the only link between Chittagong and Comilla. She prayed that not one of them would be hurt.

They needed her prayer. They had gone to the area the afternoon before, stayed in someone's home, and late at night had fitted the fuses and made everything ready. Up at 4:00 A.M., they went to finish the job.

"People think the Mukti Bahini boys were brave—but inside we were shaky," Babla admitted.

"'Let's drop the whole idea,' one of the others suggested. But, of course, we didn't. Through the rice fields we went, making sounds like wild boars. We came to the railway tracks, and a train was on the line. Bright lights—just what we didn't want. We crawled inch by inch. The two experts worked for maximum damage to the bridge. We lit the fuses—with three to five minutes for a safe retreat. On one side, the Bay of Bengal; on the other side, railway tracks and hills.

"Boom! The fuse went off. Panic gripped us. We took off like track stars. Running—not knowing where to go. No boat was available, or we would have headed out to an island. Dogs barked. Shots rang out. People swarmed toward the beach. A young fellow said he would help us, but we didn't know if we could trust him. A cry went up, 'The military is coming!'

"We were always supposed to have an emergency plan. At this time two of us hauled Razakar arm badges out of our pockets. That would protect all four of us if the military were looking for freedom fighters. But our plan backfired. The military didn't come near us, but we suddenly found ourselves surrounded by people who had spotted the Razakar badges and were out for our blood for being traitors to the Bengalis.

"I knew if they took us to the Mukti Bahini, someone there would recognize us. But it was apparent we were going to be judged by the angry mob right there. What to do? I prayed—and God saved us. Suddenly someone in the crowd recognized our leader, and he was able to convince the others that we were on the side of our people, that we were freedom fighters."

In the meantime, word of the incident had come to Chittagong. Babla's mother had heard the explosion; then someone came to tell her that two young men had been shot. The descriptions given fit two of the boys exactly. However, they had made it back to town safely, and just after the bad news reached his mother, Babla walked in the front door!

Both mother and son knew the source of their help.

"God heard all our prayers," Babla's mother said to us. "I kept a first-aid kit ready, but through all this dangerous, frightening time not one of the sixteen boys needed so much as a

Band-Aid. One did get his shirt torn, but that was all. God kept them all safe."

Listening to this account, I couldn't help feeling proud of these young Bengalis (and this mother) who had knowingly risked their lives for their country's freedom.

A story for the
missionary kids

11

A story for the missionary kids

By November, conditions were ripe for action. Many young men had returned from training in India; the freedom fighters had mobilized. The stage was set for the drama about to begin. All that remained was for the curtain to be lifted.

The eleven Americans still in Chittagong met together for Thanksgiving dinner. The U.S. government, predicting danger for us, had just sent each of us the following letter:

American Consulate General
Dacca, East Pakistan
November 24, 1971

Dear Fellow American:

After a careful evaluation of events in recent days, I am specifically recommending at this time that all dependents of U.S. citizens and all U.S. citizens whose presence in East Pakistan is not essential make their own personal arrangements to leave the province at this time.

Please bear in mind this is not a directive ordering every American to evacuate this area: It is a notice intended to prepare for eventualities should departure become advisable, and my personal recommendation that those persons specifically mentioned above make their own arrangements to leave the province via commercial facilities.

If you are a private American citizen and not an employee of the U.S. government, you should be aware of the fact that you will be ultimately responsible for your own departure in an emergency situation, but that the Consulate General stands ready to assist you in every way possible.

For the present I wish to recommend that you take the following precautionary measures:

1. Avoid unnecessary travel within or without the city.
2. Assemble your valuable documents, such as passports, securities, insurance policies, bank book, and your smaller valuable possessions such as camera, jewelry, watches.
3. Have an inventory of your personal property which you will leave behind in event of a quick departure.
4. For those of you planning to remain, we recommend that you pack a suitcase for possible eventual evacuation although, as of this date, we consider it may be necessary to "standfast" if the situation deteriorates too rapidly. At the same time, it may be prudent for you to know just what items you will wish to take with you in the event of a hurried evacuation utilizing charter or military aircraft. Under these circumstances, each family member is entitled to carry one suitcase not exceeding 40 pounds in weight.

Should you decide to leave the area now, please inform the Consular Officer so that your name may be deleted from the list of Americans now in this area. It is essential that we have current and up-to-date information on the whereabouts of all U.S. citizens.

Your cooperation and understanding is appreciated.

Sincerely,
Robert J. Carle
Consul-in-Charge

It might be good at this point for me to reiterate what I had written my family (never knowing whether they would receive mail from me in the troubled circumstances, except when a letter was carried in the U.S. diplomatic pouch and mailed by an official in Washington):

"We have a good government taking care of us."

Several times we said to each other as we were conscious of the solicitousness of consulate officials, "We'd better not meet up with any draft card burners. We'll give them an earful."

Much as we appreciated the protection of our flag, we were constantly aware that we had even a better *God* taking care of us.

On the last day in November, Mrs. Boshu and I set out for our regular Tuesday relief class. Relief was not an optional missionary activity. You *had* to be involved in relief work. To stand idly by while people starved was an impossibility. By November we had 260 families on our relief rolls. Estimating a modest six people per family, we were helping in some limited manner approximately 1,560 people. All of these lived within the city. Some were Christians whose wage earner had lost his job; some were chronically poor people who would have needed help in any situation; but the majority were Hindus whose homes had been burned to the ground or, if they were still standing, were reduced to a shell. Some, with a premonition of danger ahead, had buried money and valuables under the floors of their homes. This crime was not overlooked. The military tore up floors, digging holes in the ground underneath. We supplied clothes, blankets, towels, baby food, milk, high calorie biscuits, small amounts of tinned fish, meat, and fruit.

The class on Tuesday combined an evangelistic service with the relief distribution line. Forty women, each with at least one baby in tow, crowded into the 8x10 home of one of our believers, Menindro Das. Menindro was the Hindu convert whose relatives had spurned him for years. But now the tables had turned. In the area he was known as a Christian. A sign with a cross on it explained to the military and their stooges, "This property belongs to a Christian proprietor." Many, many people, including his own relatives, sought shelter under that sign. At one time Menindro cared for and supported thirteen girls whose lives otherwise might well have been ruined.

That Tuesday, November 30, was just like all the others. The little room was packed. The only light came from an opening in the doorway. We were all seated on the floor, although as teachers, Mrs. Boshu and I had a bamboo mat underneath us. We began by singing — the same songs over and over again because few of these women could read and must memorize the words they hear. Outside there was a babel of voices — people waiting for the religion business to get over with so they could get their quota of baby food, biscuits, and milk. Inside, the babies cried; they were passed overhead to a waiting relative in the doorway. Babies wet on the floor. In this land of no diapers, the mother calmly used her bare foot to dry up or spread out the puddle, while the rest of the people squeezed together out of the way. Old women repeated our words throughout the lesson — a polite way of showing that they were really following what we were saying.

That day we felt compelled to go back to the beginning and review the basic truths we had been stressing all these weeks: Man is sinful. God is love. God wants man to come to Him, but sin separates man from God. Jesus Christ came into the world, and by His death He removed the sin. Man is once again able to have fellowship with God. No one is able to gain this fellowship through anything that he is able to do. No amount of good works, of sacrifice of animals, flowers, or fruit, no unlimited prayer and meditation — nothing a person can do will merit salvation. Salvation is a free gift from God. By believing and receiving this free gift, man receives salvation.

So many times we had told the message, illustrating it with pictures and stories. That day we felt it was the time to ask the question: "You've heard these things many times now. What are *you* going to do about it?" There was no great response, but many walked away thoughtfully. Who can say what took place in hearts that afternoon?

On Thursday morning, December 2, between 5:00 and 6:00 A.M. the freedom fighters attacked. They had over a hundred operations planned for that early morning hour, and more than half of them were carried out. Our house shook as electric transformers and gas stations were blown to pieces. Lucy, the sixteen-year-old girl who had been living with us for a number of months, was sleeping alone in Lynn's room that night. Lynn had left to go down to the hospital for a one-day visit. Lucy decided she'd move in with me after all those explosions. If we were going to be blown up, we would go together.

Later that day the Red Cross sent us five huge gunny sacks full of clothes. We spent the rest of the day and the evening sorting, separating, and giggling at the oddities. The clothes had come just in time. We had a big distribution scheduled for the next day, and this was the finest selection of clothes we'd received yet. But during the night sound trucks blasted out the news that there was an absolute curfew throughout the country. No one could go anywhere. There was no chance to distribute clothes, no chance for Lynn to return from the hospital.

Saturday morning, December 4, we awoke to thunder! Lucy and I jumped up to look out the window. The sky was shrouded as though it were a winter blizzard. A little boy remarked, "Won't it ever be morning today?" We were just finishing breakfast at about 7:00 when we heard the sound of planes. Standing at the open verandah, we watched seven unmarked planes in perfect formation dive down in the area of the airport. We heard the violent outbursts and finally realized that the planes were from India; the smoke-filled sky was from the petrol and oil refineries which had been set ablaze as the bombers had made five concentrated raids since midnight. Antiaircraft and ground fire started up on all sides. We quickly pushed the furniture up against the walls in the living room and hauled in a mattress and sat on it.

Loudspeakers blared that the curfew would lift for a few hours at noon. This was to give people who had been unprepared time to buy food. Twelve o'clock had scarcely struck when Mr. Nundy arrived at the house scared to death. He couldn't keep his girls in the house any longer. With the curfew in force, the military had effectively shut everyone up in their houses, and the soldiers could now run rampant, breaking into homes where people had no way to get help. Could he bring his girls to me? Yes.

But before we could make any arrangements about bringing them secretly around the corner, Reid arrived. The time had come to move, he announced. We had until 2:30 to get ready; then we were all going to his house. This had been our contingency plan in case anything happened. The house was stocked with relief rice, milk, and tinned fish — a gift from the Christian Churches in Greece. (Working as we were with the International Red Cross, you had to be tri- or quad-lingual — or at least able to figure it out. We had food cases marked in Greek. Fortunately, Lynn could read Greek. Medicine came in Italian, which could be dangerous, and clothing had French labels and sizes. I gave one two-year-old a pair of pants, size 75!)

By 2:30 we were ready — Jabbor and his wife, their two

little boys, and their ten-year-old nephew, Abul, Lucy, and I
— with mattresses, sleeping bags, all the food in the house,
and valuables, which for me included the literature projects and
Lynn's Bible translation manuscripts. I drove the VW bus,
which I had never done before. I think that frightened me
as much as the threat of more bombers. Reid took the little
VW down a lane as close to the Nundy house as possible.
Quietly the girls slipped into the car. This was the first time
they had been outside since the night of March 25!

At Reid's house, rearranging and shifting the furniture that
he was storing for people who had left the country was the
first order of business. His house had suddenly become home
for twenty people. There were those of us from my house, the
three oldest Nundy girls, the three oldest Boshu girls, and Khoka
Sen's family.

Khoka had been a faithful preacher and national director of
our Bible Correspondence School for many years, but was
married to a staunch Hindu woman. In the more than ten
years since his salvation, she had never attended a church
service or shown any interest in the things of the Gospel. Eager
to keep their village home from being destroyed, she adamantly
stayed on in the village, but sent her two teen-age girls and
two little boys to live with their father on the compound where
Reid lived. All of the children became involved in the church
activities. The big girls completed the Bible correspondence
school courses and attended the day-camp program. The little
boys never missed Sunday school and sang choruses incessantly
as they followed around after Reid. Finally, when it was foolish
for her to remain in the village another day, their mother joined
them. With Khoka's two daughters, we had a dormitory of
nine girls. They chose spots on the floor and rolled out their
bedding each night.

Rather than trying to take this batch out to church on Sunday, Reid and Khoka went around to various places. In that
way a number of small neighborhood churches were held.
At our "Safe Haven" house, everyone came to the meeting,
including *Khoka's wife.*

Sunday afternoon we received a message via loudspeaker —
delivered in Urdu of course! — about what to do in case of
enemy attack. Following the oral instructions, someone came
along and gave out pamphlets with the instructions written in

Bengali. What the 75 percent of the Bengali-speaking population who are unable to read were supposed to do is anybody's guess.

The instructions told us to paste strips of brown paper over every window, dig a trench to jump into, and keep cotton batting handy to stuff into our ears. Those trenches became a city joke. The government ordered that they be dug in nearly every median dividing the road traffic and on many grassy plots. But the water level is so high that near the ocean that after just a few inches of digging you strike a swamp. Add to this the people's penchant for using the side of the road or any other convenient spot as a urinal, and you had the choice of being hit with a bomb or drowning in one of the "safe" trenches.

Set times were laid out for the compulsory curfew. At 5:30 P.M. everyone had to be inside; by 6:00 all lights had to be out. Total darkness was the law until sunrise the next morning. This made for a long, boring evening. Reid came up with a plan. Carefully cutting out cardboard to the exact size, we covered every exhaust vent and all the openings to the outside. Then we nailed two relief army blankets to each window. Fortunately, December in Chittagong is cold — otherwise we would have suffocated. Having taken these precautions, we lit one candle in the living room where we all gathered and another which was moved from the kitchen to the bathroom as needed. Reid made periodic tours around the house to be sure no light escaped.

Each evening after supper Reid led in a Bible study from the gospel of John. Those were days of unprecedented opportunity for explaining God's Word to the girls. There was no rush; we couldn't have gone anywhere if we had wanted to. The girls were free to ask questions, and they did. In private conversations with them, all three Nundy girls pointed to a time when they had accepted Christ. On the other hand, Khoka's daughters, who knew more about the cost involved in accepting Christ and especially in declaring that profession by public baptism, said they had questions that had to be answered first. They wanted to believe, but there were so many hindrances. First these had to be removed.

Western Christians are not able to understand fully the obstructions which face a convert from another religion; they are so foreign to our way of life. Problems such as: "If I become a Christian, will all of my relatives turn against me? Will I jeopardize my whole family's standing in society? Will non-Christian relatives and friends be willing to sit and eat in my house? Whom will I marry? (Really, "with whom will they arrange a marriage for me?") If my husband dies, who will take me in and support me? Who will ceremonially care for my body and bury me when I die?"

After Bible study each evening came a time when I escaped from the girls and their incessant questions and "Oh, Auntie's" and relaxed and bathed in my allotment of a bucket of hot water. Reid, meanwhile, was in constant demand to play Sorry or Peggity or Chinese Checkers.

On Monday, I drove over to our house. We had arranged for the three young men working in the Literature Division to work at the house every morning. They could tell those who needed to find me where I was and also keep up the appearance of a lived-in house. We had a man staying there all the time, but at every shot he ran down the steps and cringed under the stairwell. We still don't know whether it was he or the dog who burst through the screen door in fear!

Monday afternoon we got a chance to try out the "enemy attack" routine. The Indian bombers flew overhead, discharging their ammunition on strategic points. Only to the Bengalis, they weren't the enemy: they were the saviors, and everyone wanted to watch what they were doing and praise their skill. During that first daytime attack it was difficult to get everyone indoors and safely settled on a mattress in the middle of the living room floor. Reid was at the office where all the staff and inquirers were out on the lawn watching the show.

Tuesday and Wednesday we had a visitor in our hostel: our fellow missionary Mel Beals drove up from the hospital. Sixty-five miles away from the city, the folks at Memorial Christian Hospital had seen the smoke from the initial fires and didn't know if we and all of the city were in flames or not. Mel brought with him a welcome note from Lynn. Actually, Lynn had vacillated before deciding to make the trip to Malumghat. Her purpose is going was to meet with Mrs. Dass, newly returned from seven months of hiding in Burma. Lynn was anxious to resume the long interrupted work on the Bible translation and needed to confer with Mrs. Dass first. She wrote:

Tuesday, Dec. 7

Dear Jeannie,

Hi! Sure miss you and wonder what you're doing and how things are in town. Thus far it has been obvious God wanted me to stay here, as there's been no way to get into Chittagong. I debated about going with Mel, but it's uncertain whether he'll get there or not so I think I should stay here. I'd come in a minute if I knew my presence there would be of any help. Let me know if it is and I'll come at the next opportunity.

There's been bombing of one kind or another at Cox's Bazar during the night and this morning.

Sure hope I can get there by your birthday. Or maybe you should come down here so we can celebrate it in style. In case we aren't together, I thought I'd send this little thing for you.

I've written this very quickly so that I can get it to Mel.

Love,
Lynn

During the two days Mel was in town, there was a lull in the fighting. Everything was, as one American expressed it, "quite normal for an abnormal situation." There was no bombing or shooting during those two days. Mel was a bit disappointed that he'd have no war stories to tell his kids when he got back to the hospital.

His work finished, Mel went to pick up a jeep that a Malumghat neighbor wanted taken to the hospital for safekeeping, only to be told that no gasoline was available for civilians. Changing his plans, he booked a seat on the earliest possible bus going towards the hospital. Then his adventure began. Mel tells it like this:

"The ride was fine until we reached the halfway point between Chittagong and Malumghat; then the Pakistan military signaled for the driver to halt. They told him to clear the bus as they intended using it. We could deduce from the row of parked buses and trucks that they were confiscating everything that came along.

"We all got off the bus. I prayed that somehow God would let me get back to the hospital without further delay; I didn't want my family to be upset. Scarcely had I finished praying when there in front of me was our hospital ambulance. What an answer to prayer! The driver explained that he had one call to make about twenty miles away; then he would return and we could go back together.

"I sat down to wait and got into conversation with a *Mulvie* (a religious teacher of Islam). Sitting in a tea shop, my friend and I listened to the Pakistan military discussing assaults which had been made against them by the Mukti Bahini. The name of the town they mentioned was exactly where our ambulance was heading.

"By late afternoon when our ambulance still hadn't returned, I explained my problem to the Pakistan major. He considered the matter and offered me a jeep to drive to the hospital. Then he changed his mind and said, 'No, I'd better not do that. I'll give you one of the buses I've stopped.'

"My Mulvie friend and I climbed aboard the bus. En route the driver picked up other passengers. All along the road there were squadrons of military and the military's band of Bengali traitors — the hated Razakars.

"Entering a small town, our bus was stopped by a group of armed men. Thinking this group to be a band of Razakars, I explained that I was from the hospital and that *their* major had given me this bus to get home.

"'*Our* major?' they asked. 'What major? What was his name?'

"'I don't know his name,' I answered. 'But if you have a phone, we can call him and you will see that I am telling you the truth.'

"'We're not going to phone anyone,' they replied. 'You come and sit over here.'

"I was getting angry by this time. Retrieving my packages from the bus, I called to them, 'Why are you treating me like this? Why don't you obey your own commander's orders? I want to know what this is all about before I will go and sit down.'

"'Then we'll have to put you under arrest.' And with that they called for rope to tie me up.

"Just then a car appeared down the road. The armed men ran to their positions leaving one young man to guard me. To ease my mind until I could clear up this whole mess, I began talking to the friendly boy who was my guard. Suddenly I took a good look at him. He was wearing a uniform shirt of a kind I'd never seen before. On the shoulder was a strap-type thing that wasn't buttoned. Gingerly I flipped it up. There under the strap was the green and red symbol of the Bangladesh government. These boys weren't Razakars at all; they were freedom fighters! I was among friends!

"Quickly I explained the whole problem. Talking in Bengali, I told how I had mistaken them for Razakars and naturally thought they would be under the orders of the Pakistan major. The young guard smiled, hugged me, and shook my hand. Then the leader returned. Hearing the story, he invited me to their camp as their guest.

"In the meantime, the Mukti Bahini had captured twenty-eight men. Some were Bihari businessmen who had collaborated with the military; some were tribal people working with the civil armed forces of the Pakistani army. They tied these men up and put us all back on the same bus. I was up front as the honored guest. Suddenly I realized the danger I was in. As we blasted down the road, I thought, *Great snakes, what if we run into a military patrol. They'll just riddle this bus, and I'll be the prime target.*

"Ten miles back up the road towards Chittagong, we switched from the bus into cars for the five-mile trip into the hills where the freedom fighters' camp was located. We entered a heavily guarded gate and were stopped several times by freedom fighters challenging us as to who we were. Finally in the camp, I met an old friend, a Christian man from Chittagong. This helped in further establishing my identity.

"After a delicious meal, they gave me a place to sleep — a mat on the dirt floor of an empty school. In the middle of the night, the group leader whose spot I had preempted returned.

"'Who's in my bed? Who gave my spot away?' he shouted.

"As I got up the next morning, the guerrilla fighters were lined up before the flagpole going through drill routines. Then just as the sun broke through, the flag of Bangladesh was raised to the tingling accompaniment of shouts of 'Joi Bangla!' It brought tears to my eyes to watch the enthusiasm of the Bengalis finally getting what they'd suffered and fought for so long.

"The next activity of the morning I did not want to witness; I did not want it etched on my memory. The twenty-eight men

who had been taken prisoner were executed for willingly as-
sisting the enemy military regime.

"At mid-morning, other officers talked to my Mulvie friend
and me. They told us we were free to leave if we wanted to,
but that we could ride with a patrol going on maneuvers in
an hour or so. We said we would pass up that great opportunity and find a rickshaw out to the main road.

"We shook hands, and they apologized for the inconvenience
they had caused us. As is the custom, I replied, 'Oh, you
haven't given me any trouble. We enjoyed our night's stay
with you, and we hope to see you again someday.'"

Rather later than he had intended, Mel rejoined his worried
family and the equally anxious missionary staff at Malumghat.
He *had* a story to tell his kids when he got home.

Joi Bangla at last

12

Joi Bangla at last

The brief lull in hostilities in Chittagong brought out people who had been terrorized into staying indoors. Some took this opportunity to seek me out at my house. A number wanted to know where there was a place they could safely find shelter; others wanted relief goods.

Months before, we had made the decision to take the relief supplies — food, clothing, blankets, etc. — out to where the people lived rather than having them constantly at the door, but that plan didn't work! People had a way of finding the house. Instead of doing their work, the literature staff spent most of the time directing or escorting the people over to "Safe Haven" (Reid's house). One person needed baby food; one needed payment for sewing work she had done; another was unable to pay his house rent and needed a loan until companies would start paying salaries again.

Thursday morning, December 9, I received a note from the men working at my house.

> "Dear Sister. Please come at 11:00 A.M. We've told a family to come back then. They have the sickest child we've ever seen."

I went at 11:00 A.M., but the family didn't show up. Just moments before, however, another note had arrived from the Nundys around the corner.

> "Please come immediately. Mr. Nundy has had a heart attack."

I went at once and found a very sick man. His breathing was labored; his pulse and blood pressure were irregular. This was no job for a mere nurse. Again God's perfect timing! Before the curfew began, Drs. Peter and Reba MacField had returned from their sojourn in Burma, bringing with them three-month-old Shancitra, little "Bubbly." They were attempting to get up to Dacca and on north to their families, but the outbreak of war prevented all travel. They were staying in our mission guest house along with a newly married couple who had arrived in East Pakistan on the last possible civilian flight out of Karachi. Andrew Akand had come to begin work as Office Manager, but first had to spend his time supporting his bride who quite naturally had "heart failure" every time a rocket was blasted from the police station next door.

Was this the same Dr. Peter we had met at Malumghat back in April? No, this man was a "new creature in Christ," a man who had made his peace with God, a man who had exchanged his intellectual doubts for the sure foundation of faith. But there was no time to hear about that experience now. We had to hurry to Mr. Nundy's house. We started him on a regimen of rest and tranquilizers. There was no possibility of hospitalization or diagnostic tests. Even taking the doctor to see him was risky business. The military needed doctors for their mounting wounded, and doctors had been known to step out of their homes and never be heard of again. We decided that either Reid or I would take Dr. Peter as often as it was necessary for him to see Mr. Nundy.

Later that same afternoon, Reid took the doctor over—the two of them riding on the Honda. Suddenly the street seemed to empty of even the few people who were out walking. Peter tapped Reid on the shoulder and shouted, "Where is everybody?" Before he got the words out, that afternoon's contingent of planes appeared and began dropping their deadly load. "Everybody" had ducked into shelter—everybody, that is, except the two on the Honda who hadn't heard the roar of the bombers' engines.

Friday at 3:00 A.M. we heard the roar of planes coming closer and closer. Perhaps every sound was just intensified during the night hours, or perhaps they really did circle right overhead. Then two enormous blasts shook the solid brick and

cement house. I was sleeping in a storage area, with a door
opening into the living room where the girls were asleep, wall-
to-wall. My bed was wedged between a tall metal cupboard at
the head and a dresser at the foot. In my semi-awake state, I
was sure the vibrations from the blast would cause that huge
cupboard to fall over on my head. I held on to the bed and
prayed those planes away.

Our first activity every morning was listening to the news:
BBC at six o'clock and Voice of America at seven. That Friday
all the stations reported that the capital city, Dacca, was surrounded by Indian forces and would fall in a matter of days.
Evacuation planes were unable to get into Dacca to take out
those who wished to leave. (Those planes would not have done
us any good; we couldn't have gotten to Dacca.)

Two ships left Chittagong after the war began with a total
of fifty-one foreigners aboard. The first one carried friends of
ours who had been with a business concern and with CARE.
We didn't know about the second ship until it had gone, but it
was no one's fault that we had not been informed. They knew
we had decided to stay. The die was cast when we accepted
responsibility for the girls.

One of my lovely memories from our days at "Safe Haven"
was the solicitousness of the girls for what they sensed we must
be feeling. How often this concern came out in their prayers
as they prayed that our families in the United States would not
be unduly worried about us. The girls were well aware that
mail was at a standstill, both incoming and outgoing, and long-
distance telephone had never been a viable means of communication in Chittagong. Now even emergency overseas cables
were, at the best, unpredictable.

I recall the day one of the girls prayed that word would reach
our families *in time for Christmas*. How happy I was later on
when I could tell her that my cable saying

ALL SAFE. HAPPY CHRISTMAS. STOP. JEANNIE

had arrived in Stony Brook, New York, on December 23 (when
it was already Christmas Eve in Bangladesh).

By Saturday, December 11, we all needed a break from the
routine of cooking, cleaning, and remaking used clothing into
useful sizes. We invited Dr. Peter and his wife and the Akands

over for a visit. For a few hours we forgot the war while we played games, sang Christmas carols, and made ice cream in the hand freezer.

That was the last day we were able to let the girls enjoy themselves out in the yard. The Pakistani military stationed antiaircraft guns on the tops of a number of neighboring houses. This meant they could look right down into the yard where the girls had been sitting. We warned them to be quieter and stopped them from listening to the still clandestine Radio Bangladesh. Just before curfew time, at five in the evening, the Indian army planes returned. The antiaircraft guns were in working order by then, with the result that the entire sky above us was a mass of white puffs. They looked like floating balloons, but the puffs were really the smoke which concealed the dangerous shrapnel that fell after each shot.

Sunday morning we had just sat down to eat breakfast, when boom-boom-boom—the planes were back. This time we didn't even bother to leave the table.

"Oh, Auntie," one of the girls cried. Then, "Pass the bananas." You really do get acclimated to the noise of the bombs and shots!

Again that Sunday we all stayed in our homes with the preachers going around to pray and encourage the people at various homes. All of our household came to the meeting, along with the parents of two of the girls who brought news of their own families. Reid and Khoka had left for an afternoon meeting when the planes started in with great furor. The following afternoon at the same time we were surrounded with the storms from the planes. I had just made the comment, "Maybe we'll get a cup of tea in peace today," when the racket started up again.

Those were busy days. I organized the group into work crews. The youngest ones swept and washed the floors; middle-sized ones did the dishes; older ones helped Jabbor with the cooking.

For breakfast we ate puffed rice and bananas—"home grown" —or a flat bread quite a bit like a pancake. Lunch and supper were carbon copies: Rice—ten cups of uncooked rice for each meal; a split-pea-like gravy which was poured over the rice; a vegetable chopped up and fried in spices; and either fish or eggs and even, once or twice, *chicken*.

Reid's garden was on its last legs, but we gleefully picked and hoarded ears of corn until there was enough for everyone to try out this novelty. They didn't like it! But in scrounging between the rows the girls found what we thought were weeds—that's how much *we* knew about it. It was a kind of wild spinach, which combined with the tinned fish made quite a tasty combination.

On days when it seemed safe, Jabbor went to shop in the bazaar. There was little merchandise available since the farmers and suppliers had no way of getting their products into the city. Sometimes he was able to bring back some vegetables—a few beans, eggplant, and the inevitable pumpkin. These the girls took outside to the area behind the kitchen door. Holding a large knife between their big toe and second toe, they steadied it on the ground. That left both hands free to slice up the vegetables.

Besides the routine chores, I suggested that the girls keep diaries of those eventful days in their lives.

Tuesday, December 14, is a day that will live in my memory. It was my birthday, and I awoke to more than a twenty-one-gun salute! Getting dressed in the bathroom, I had to keep ducking under the washbowl to get out of the direct range of the rattling windows. It's a little difficult to get dressed squatting under a sink, doubled over, with your stomach in your mouth. When that barrage had passed and I was able to get out to the living/dining room, I found that the girls had gathered flowers into a bouquet and a lei for me; Khoka's wife had prepared a special kind of rice, raisin, and banana dish for our breakfast; and Khoka led in a song and prayer. Later in the day I drove the two miles to my house where the three young men and I decided to shut down the literature operation there—the danger factor was high and the concentration factor low.

Back at Reid's house, I found that the girls had prepared another birthday surprise. They had spent a good part of the day mixing and rolling out a sort of sweet pastry-strip. They used up most of our carefully stored cooking oil, and the strips took so long to fry that they wasted more kerosene in the stove than we usually used for a meal, but I didn't ever have the heart to tell them that. Actually, we were rationing out the kerosene and trying to use an electric immersion heater and a small rice cooker for as many things as we could stretch our imaginations to include. The thought of uncooked food didn't bother anyone nearly as much as the day it became clear that we had been using too much water. The tank went dry and the septic tank got full.

Bengalis are great bathers. Normally, the faucets along the roadsides are crowded with men and children merrily scrubbing away. For many, the daily bath before the noontime meal is practically a religious rite; unless they bathe, they won't eat. Our having to decree that there could be no baths struck most of them harder than any of the other restrictions.

Mrs. Boshu and the quaint little old Didi-Ma came to visit on the afternoon of my birthday. The reports they had been hearing were bad: Terrible fighting in Dacca, with the word that there would never be a surrender; the Pakistan military would fight to the last man there, then move on to take Chittagong. If there was any chance that Pakistan would be defeated, they were prepared to destroy everyone and everything before the downfall. The non-Bengali population had been armed and were going from house to house looting, plundering, and destroying people and property. Truth and rumor were hard to separate, but Mrs. Boshu must have felt that the end had come. She went from person to person hugging them and crying a little before she ran to catch a bicycle rickshaw for the ride home.

The radio was full of the news that the Seventh Fleet had been moved into the Bay of Bengal. As far as we Americans were concerned, that was our moment of greatest fear. Now, even our loyal friends looked at us suspiciously. According to them, the United States, long upheld as a citadel of freedom, had failed the Bengalis in their hour of need. Not only had they refused to recognize Bangladesh and come to her aid, but they actually had supplied the weapons and conveyances which the enemy used to rain death upon the Bengali race. And then when India stepped in to end the massacre, the United States turned nuclear warships against her! Never had anti-American feeling been more intense.

John P. Lewis, one-time U.S. AID director in India (1964-69) and now dean of the Woodrow Wilson School of Public and International Affairs at Princeton, wrote in the *New York Times*:

We have managed to align ourselves with the wrong side of about as big and as simple a moral issue as the world has seen lately; and we have sided with a minor military dictatorship against the world's second largest nation. [1]

In Britain, the conservative *London Daily Telegraph* accused Washington of "a blundering diplomatic performance which can have few parallels." [2]

As American citizens living in East Pakistan and aware of what was going on, we wrote our president expressing our sympathy with the just cause of the Bengalis.

On Thursday morning, December 16, we listened to the radio as Bhutto, Pakistan's special envoy to the United Nations, walked out of the Security Council because no one was helping his country. He complained of "delaying action" while Dacca fell into Indian hands. After the days of regular heavy attacks both from the planes and ground fire, that morning seemed still as a cemetery. One of the few foreign businessmen left in the city came to check on our welfare. He was working full time with the Red Cross during those days and told dreadful tales of rescue operations out in the dock areas where the heaviest bombing had been. Many ships had suffered direct hits, and even foreign ships had been sunk.

Reid and I volunteered to help with the Red Cross work in any way possible. We learned that the manager of the only western-style hotel in the city had opened his doors to make the hotel available to the Red Cross for whatever purpose they chose. He was not just being philanthropic; he was a practical man who knew that enormous red crosses flying on top of the largest building in the city might be the only thing that would save his hotel. We were told that we could move in there and live and eat free as long as the emergency lasted. (Rather than cheering the populace, the absence of the planes overhead seemed to be a premonition of a worse kind of battle—the hand-to-hand street blood bath that everyone felt was in store for Chittagong.) We thanked the Red Cross people for letting us know about this possibility but decided that the girls would be safer ducking under the overturned furniture in the living room than they

---

[1] Fazlul Quader Quaderi, ed., *Bangladesh GENOCIDE and World Opinion*, p. 289.

[2] *Ibid.*

would being exposed to the crews from stranded ships and the variety of other people crowded into the hotel.

Late that Thursday afternoon, the nearest neighbors called across to ask us to open up the gate between the two compounds. They had heard rumors that a cease-fire had been declared in Dacca and were afraid of a last-ditch stand here. They wanted to send their women over to our house if violence broke out.

I kept the possibility of the cease-fire to myself, not wanting to get the girls' hopes up over a rumor. The minute Reid arrived, I directed him across to the neighbor's to find out what that man knew. Then we traveled the radio dial trying to see if what he had said was true. We could not get any direct news until 7:15 that evening when Mrs. Indira Gandhi announced: "Dacca is a free capital of a free country. We hail the people of Bangladesh in their hour of triumph!"

The girls burst out crying.

Khoka broke into the Doxology and then led in prayer.

Reid sneaked away to a well-hidden box from which he uncovered the green, red, and gold flag of Bangladesh. We turned on the forbidden lights and set up the flag in a place of honor.

Piecing together the bits of news available, we learned that at 12:15 Pakistan General Niazi had surrendered unconditionally to the Indian army. The information was delayed in reaching Chittagong because earlier in the week the Indian Air Force had scored a direct hit on the only remaining radio transmitter left in the city. They had not meant to hit the transmitter, but had received false information that a particular railway office housed a military installation. The military had moved away, but the air raid wiped out all possibility of contact outside of Chittagong.

Pakistani officers and soldiers also heard of the cease-fire via the international news media. That is, some of them heard the news; others were listening to President Yahya Khan's declaration that East Pakistan still wanted to be an integral part of Pakistan. He stated that the fighting would continue—that one setback did not decide a whole war.

Many took his advice and continued the fighting long and loud throughout that night. As morning broke there were cries, shouts, shots, and bursts of fire. We weren't sure if this was war or victory, and we huddled for the last time under the tables and overturned living room sofa and chairs.

By 10:00 A.M. the city was wild. Everyone had heard the true news of the cease-fire. The streets which had been bleak and empty burst into life. Suddenly every roadway was jammed with people. Cars, buses, and trucks so long left idle were filled with people of all ages. Women threw back their face coverings and danced in the streets. Everyone shouted "Joi Bangla" until they were hoarse.

And then the *saviors*—the Indian army—arrived. As truckload after truckload passed by, Bengalis lining the streets wept, cheered, and called to them. Any Indian soldier brave enough to get down from his transport was engulfed by local people wanting to touch him, to talk to him, to express appreciation. The change in the attitude of the people was dramatic. Children who had run from the sight of a military uniform now climbed into the soldiers' arms. Women were treated with respect. This was freedom, and the Bengalis basked in it.

"Joi Bangla!" was in the very air of Golden Bengal, as her poets have called her.

Recollection

13

Recollection

The war was over, but its victims—those who survived, that is—needed care. My part, since I had volunteered to work with the Red Cross, was, along with Dr. Peter, to set up an emergency hospital on the second floor of the hotel. To get the necessary supplies there we had to drive many miles around the city.

In order to protect ourselves from a city gone mad, we sacrificed pillowcases and the cloth from a red relief skirt to make Red Cross flags. I was proud of our efforts and was tying them onto improvised flagpoles on both cars when Reid came to inspect them. He took one look at the pillowcase crosses and complained, "You've made Christian crosses. Red Cross crosses are equal in length on all four extensions."

The girls and I started over again and soon had passable replicas of the international symbol. But then I turned the corner of the driveway too sharply and broke my car's flagpole in half. The blunt nose of my VW bug will always bear the marks of the adhesive tape with which my Red Cross flag was finally anchored.

While I treated gunshot wounds, soothed lost children, and bandaged those who had been savagely beaten, Reid organized and worked in the Missing Persons Bureau. Hundreds of names were submitted — few were ever located. Each heartrending tale had a similar ring: a knock on the door late at night; the men of the house marched away and never heard of again; a phony order to report at some official residence—the appointment was with death.

Areas that had been "off-limits" for the past nine months were opened and inspected. What did this reveal?

The impressive Circuit House that had once proudly housed Queen Elizabeth II had become a hole of horrors. A search brought to light instruments of torture, firing lines, and mass graves.

A beautiful lakeside park where we held our Sunday school picnics was clogged with the mutilated bodies of girls used and discarded by the troops.

Sewers were choked with bloated, decaying bodies. In various places around our city there were shallow graves full of skeletons picked clean by jackals and vultures.

No one could stop talking. The months of silence had been hard for the volatile, voluble Bengalis. Now each wanted to tell his story. We heard of Christians interrupted in the middle of their worship service. They were marched out of the church and lined up on one side of a ditch, while Hindu neighbors lined the other side. The Hindus were shot and toppled into the ditch.

We heard about a girl who was snatched from her grandmother's protection and forced into a jeep headed for the army barracks. Somehow she convinced the driver that she needed a drink of water. Running into a hotel, she begged the proprietor to save her. Bravely he hid her and helped her escape. The military beat him and finally drove him away to certain death because he refused to disclose where the girl was.

A man was admitted to our hospital with his face eaten away and his lips in shreds; soldiers had thrown acid on him because he would not give up his daughter. Do you understand why we had been so concerned for our girls?

Those who had fled from the city told of living on leaves and roots as they walked for fifteen nights over hills and through muddy fields and rough trails. Some told of families who were unable to carry all of their children. Those too heavy to be held yet too young to walk were set by the side of the road, given a biscuit, and told that their mothers would come back. They never did!

The daily newspaper carried poignant accounts such as this one entitled "Glimpses of the Days of Our Exile," by C. R. Das, Advocate:

"They were part of another caravan that started the long trek in quest of safety and shelter. There was the eighty-two-year-old mother, her son and daughter-in-law, along with about two thousand victims of the Pak army barbarity, when the whole village was razed to the ground and burnt and many killed.

"Two days of continuous walking through high hills and arduous terrain had made the old mother completely exhausted. She could not move any more, but safety and shelter were still more than a day away.

"It was the evening of 16 April 1971. The old lady was leaning against a tree. She waved to her son and daughter-in-law to come nearer and told them, with tears rolling down her wrinkled cheeks, 'I can't make it any more. Leave me here and you move on.' She was gasping for breath.

"The son and daughter-in-law vehemently protested and so did the others. They could not leave her there alone. But the old lady stopped them, saying, 'Don't be fools. This is no time for sentiment. I have lived my life. You are young. Think of your children and their future in Bangladesh. Leave me here. The enemy forces will start their "search and destroy" business again in the morning. They are not far off. Go away and leave me alone.' She was too tired to speak any more.

"With heavy hearts they agreed. She was leaning against the tree and looking at the not-too-distant hill where the sun was setting. They put a pot of water and some puffed rice beside her. One by one, with tears, they took leave of her. The old lady was mumbling blessings over them.

"No one knows what happened to her; perhaps no one ever will. She was from the ravaged village of Raozan in Chittagong."

Some of the stories held a twist of humor. In Dacca there is a famous old Hindu temple, a tourist attraction. Early in the Hindu purge, the temple priests were killed. When the military wanted to propagate its lie that "everything was normal," that there had been no pogrom against any class of people, they devised this scheme: they dressed up rank and file soldiers as

Hindu priests and ordered them to sit on the temple steps and meditate. The military proudly brought foreign journalists to inspect: "see for yourselves." Things were going according to plan until the senior officers came on the scene. Then every "Hindu priest" snapped to attention and saluted the superior officers!

Once again we were anxious to learn what had happened to all of our friends. The godly pastor of the British Baptist Church, his wife, and their two teen-age daughters had lived on a crowded street in the heart of Chittagong throughout the trouble.

Rev. Sardar explained, "We didn't have the money to pay the prices asked to get any kind of conveyance to take a family out of the city. We had to stay. We read the Old Testament account of the children of Israel who spread the blood on the doorposts of their houses and were saved from death." Dramatically pointing to the doorway, he continued, "We claimed that blood for our protection too. The military passed by many, many times, but God blinded their eyes."

Nikhil Sarkar was the last of our church young people whom we located. Nikhil himself is a baptized believer, but the rest of his family are Hindus. All of them fled to safety in a remote village, leaving Nikhil in the home of a college friend. As middle-class business people, Nikhil's family had a good home and a prosperous shop. The home was looted and stripped of every single item—even family portraits that could be of no value to anyone else. Just before Christmas we received a note from a Calcutta hospital:

> Early in December I tried to escape from the city in the company of about a hundred men. We were attacked by a band of traitorous men hired by the military to shoot Hindus. I took a bullet in my back and my leg. A friend carried me eight or nine miles to the border, where the Indian army gave me first aid and arranged for me to be brought to this hospital.
>
> I hope to return soon.
>
> In Christ,
> Nikhil

Mrs. Dass returned to the city to begin putting her house in order after its months as a Mukti Bahini hideout. We wept and rejoiced with her as we finally heard how they had fared throughout the past nine months.

She had good cause to fear what might happen had she remained in Chittagong. Just two weeks before she and her husband left (their daughter Rachel already had gone with us to Malumghat), Mrs. Dass had been asked to speak to a group of women about the issues facing them as a nation.

"Mujib's cause was just," Mrs. Dass states, "and I was a hundred percent for him. Some of the women wanted to march to show they were pro-Mujib. Because many of these women had been my own pupils, they insisted that they could not walk ahead of me, their teacher. So I was given a banner and walked at the head of the procession. Many people heard and joined their teacher."

This incident marked Mrs. Dass. Add to this the atrocities being perpetrated against Hindus, the molesting of women, and Mr. and Mrs. Dass had ample reason for fleeing to Malumghat.

"We arrived at Malumghat where Lynn and Jeannie, the Ketchams, the Olsens, and so many of our friends were.

"Dr. Olsen said, 'You have come to a peaceful place. No one will harm you here; you have come home.'"

Mr. and Mrs. Dass were still at Malumghat when we made our hasty retreat through Burma. We were eager to hear the rest of their story.

"Many people were flocking to Malumghat for refuge. But on April 23, Dr. Ketcham and Dr. Olsen came to tell us that the army was advancing and we would have to leave to preserve our lives, for the military was ruthlessly hunting and killing. The two doctors were in tears as they told us we must leave.

"Dr. Olsen had been making arrangements for the hospital employees, many of them Hindu, to be taken to the mission's jungle station, Hebron, when the motorcycle accident happened. With his arm broken, he kept on making these arrangements.

"By this time four others had joined us, all doctors: Dr. and Mrs. Peter MacField and two Muslim doctors. We were eleven in all as we started out for Burma, intending to cross into India where I have a brother and sister and many other relatives.

"I will never forget that scene as we left Malumghat. *Would we ever meet again?* was the question in our minds. Dr.

Ketcham was so moved at our departing that he had to walk away from us and weep and weep.

"Thousands of refugees were pouring into Burma from Chittagong and the south. Because we were educated professional people, we were given accommodation in a government rest house, but only for one week. After that all eleven of us lived together in a thatched house.

"Dr. Ketcham had given each refugee leaving the hospital one hundred rupees. We were so grateful for this kindness. For one month only, the Burmese government supplied us with rice. We were there for seven months, for we were not permitted to cross into India or even to communicate with our family there.

"It was during those days I learned to know God in ways I had never known Him before. We were sick, some suffering from bloody dysentery. We were hungry. We sent runners to Malumghat with letters to Dr. Ketcham telling him of our plight, but months went by and never a reply. We later learned that he had answered every one of our letters and had sent money and supplies to us, but the runners had stolen everything he ever sent to us.

"The day came when we had only five rupees left. I prayed, 'Lord, send us help if you want us to stay here.'

"Lynn had written her mother and given her our address in the refugee camp in Burma; she also gave her mother my brother's address in India. Lynn's mother sent money to us, and through Lynn's mother my brother was able to send us money in two separate letters (in case one was lost). It took a long time to have the check and international money order released to us, but we finally got it.

"I wrote the Burmese Bible Society asking that they pray for us. I had had contact with them in our translation work and had met some of them when Lynn and I attended a translators' conference in Bangkok. Praise God, they prayed and also ministered to our physical needs. In all they sent us seven hundred rupees. God had us in His hands.

"At this time while God was mindful of our desperate situation, Satan was not letting me alone. Thoughts that now make me ashamed crowded into my mind. *Why had the missionaries forsaken us? Why didn't they reply to my letters?* I wrestled with this deep inner concern until it came to me that I must go back. I was praying and praying about this. Then came the first letter from Malumghat — Mr. Walsh's letter. 'Come back,' he wrote. 'We will take care of you.'

"But to get back! I determined I must go. 'Even if they kill me,' I said. For we were hearing of people who had tried to return to East Pakistan and were killed. The two Muslim doctors decided to stay and the other nine — no, ten of us, for the MacField baby had been born in Burma — started for the border.

"Mr. Walsh sent us two hundred rupees by a runner, and we received this! What a part it played in our getting back to Malumghat! But before that there were other dangers ahead of us. We had so hoped that Mr. Walsh or someone else from Malumghat could meet us at the border, but due to a tense situation they could not do this. They did make every possible arrangement for our safety. Many returning refugees had been invited to 'reception centers' where they were beaten, then killed.

"We managed to cross the Burma border into East Pakistan at a point where only a canal separates the two countries. Once on the other side, however, there was no conveyance available. Several buses came along, but they wouldn't take us. How we prayed! And God answered — along came an empty bus. The driver was willing to take us, for thanks to the missionaries' provision of the two hundred rupees, we could pay him what he asked. He told us, however, that he had one bad tire, and if it went flat we would have to wait about two hours while he fixed it. What if it happened in an exposed area? What if the Pak military came on the scene? They would kill us. They had been looking for me, I knew.

We decided to take the chance and trust the Lord to take care of us. We felt He had sent along this empty bus — a most unusual thing. Mile after mile the Lord kept that tire going. Then our fears were realized. We were stopped by the Punjabi police! They asked where we were going.

"'To Malumghat,' we replied.

"'Are you all patients?' they persisted.

"I answered, 'No, I work with the missionaries there.'

"'You can't go there,' they said. 'You have to go back to Cox's Bazar.'

"Go back! That meant only one thing. They would kill all of us. But God had us in His hands. Just then my husband stepped over toward a little shelter, and there were two Bengali police. My husband offered them five rupees. They interceded for us, and the Punjabis let us go! The tire did blow later, but by then we were in a secluded spot.

"I will never forget our arrival at Malumghat. What joy for us and our dear friends as we talked about how God had kept all of us in His hands! We kept hearing of the awful things that were happening in Dacca and in Chittagong. Lynn came 'for one day' so that we could talk about our translation work and rejoice with each other, but conditions were such that she was unable to return to Chittagong. I was praying and crying to the Lord, 'O God! What has my country done? Will you not free my people?' And after just one week — *freedom!*"

In adding to this story, Dr. Peter MacField confessed, "Remember how I said I was going to experiment with this praying business? Well, I did. And I learned that prayer is a most extraordinary affair:

> We prayed for God to send us money — He sent it just when we really needed it.
> We prayed for God to spare our lives — We could have been captured and killed on various occasions. God saved us.
> We prayed for God to take us back safely — In spite of obstacles, God did.

"Personally, I saw the power of prayer when on September 1 our baby was born. There we were, far from home. We had enough medical personnel to be sure — three doctors and one midwife, not counting the patient herself, a doctor — but no equipment of any kind should anything have gone wrong. Besides that, we had no supplies for the baby. Generously, Burmese Christians outside the refugee camp provided everything we needed: clothes and a little bowl for the baby's bath. The baby is fat and healthy, and my wife is strong and able to nurse the baby well.

"In all these ways the grace of God was revealed to me in such a way that I cannot doubt Him. I want to spend my life in serving Him."

One day I asked our lovely Lucy, "Did you ever finish writing up your thoughts about this year — the diary you were writing while we were at Mr. Minich's house?"

Rather shyly she answered, "Yes, I finished it. Do you want to read it?"

I did — and I think you will want to read it, too.

Lucy had entitled her diary:

RECOLLECTION

Sad is the memory of the year 1971, but great the reward!

On March 26 we could hear bursting of bombs and the shooting of guns. Struck with fear, I called my mother. She too was frightened and called my father. He said to go back to sleep in peace. He said that civil war had started. Still our eyes lit with fear as we stared in the darkness.

March 27 we could see people on foot with small amounts of luggage and food heading for the villages as they thought it was not safe for them to stay in the town. During the night everything seemed peaceful and calm. We were about to climb to bed — and all of a sudden we heard firing of machine guns. My father came out. Oh, he was shocked as he saw red and yellow lights flowing over the roof. We were all called by my father to run for shelter between our back wall and my cousin's house.

Then on March 29 we passed the day in peace. At three o'clock, seven truckloads moved slowly along the road and up to a hill at the back of our house. My father watched from afar. One of the soldiers walked up to a man who was heading for home. Without asking him any questions, he slapped the man right and left. Another soldier bent over our wall and asked my father, "What are you?"

My father answered, "I'm a *Christian.*"

"Go inside," the soldier ordered.

We stayed here for two or three days. Then my father decided it was impossible to stay so close with the soldiers just on the back hill, so we moved not far away. With the Lord's help we crossed safely under the very noses of the soldiers to a two-story building where, with three more families, we stayed for three months. During this time the difficulties we went through were intolerable: no lights, markets closed, no water, etc. We used to draw water from a nearby well, filter it, then drink it. We had to bathe after three or four o'clock due to the scarcity of water. During this time there was no radio news. The news which we heard from the mouths of the people was quite true: Abducting young girls, looting, killing, burning houses — all these took place. During this time my heart cried out for our Bengalis. *What will happen to us?*

I simply lost the hope for victory. I thought about myself. *I am a young girl. What will happen to me? It is better to die than that these things happen to us.* Then I prayed to the Lord and said, "You are the One who created us and You know what is best for us. You are my only refuge and shelter." This prayer consoled me very much.

Then the country seemed to be in a normal state. Schools and offices opened with the command of the government. My school reopened, but I did not go as my father thought young girls should not come out of the house.

Things became worse by the day. I went to stay with Jeannie Lockerbie and Lynn Silvernale. I joined school in the month of October as I thought I shouldn't delay my education as it is the backbone of our nation.

During this time the freedom fighters did not give way for the enemies, though they were still not strong with sufficient arms and ammunition. Once coming home from school, just as we turned a corner we saw people running and shops being closed as quickly as possible. We guessed what was the matter and asked the driver. He said, "a bomb bursted." Just as we turned our car for another route home, I caught a glimpse of a young man lying in a footpath, his clothes red with blood.

The freedom fighters were getting stronger. They were desperate in their work and determined they would fight to the last in order to gain independence. With so much punishment, still our young fighters continued.

Then on December 4 about seven o'clock we heard planes flying and what sounded like thunder. At first I thought it was thunder as the day was cloudy. Aunt Jeannie said planes were bombing near the jetty. There was nothing for us to do but pray to the Lord and take shelter. A curfew was set up, and the bombing stopped about nine o'clock. Nature was sailing graciously: the wild west wind was blowing and the cloudiness melted away with the appearance of the sun. The city was calm and quiet and peaceful except for a few soldiers on the road. I lost myself in thought; I felt very lonely and desolate.

At noon the curfew was withdrawn. Mr. Minich came, and they decided that we should go and stay in his house. There were eight other girls. All this time bombing took place nearly every day at tea time—three o'clock. Either it would come just before tea or just after tea. If anyone was outside, they ran inside the house, and everyone lay down on the floor.

The night bombing was longer; it was very serious. The house shook, and we heard the windows cracking. Fear struck me. Nothing came out of my mouth but a whisper, "Lord, protect us."

Our daily food was rice and curry and tinned fish. We were tired of it, but it was better than nothing. Thanks to those who sent it.

On December 16 a neighbor wanted to see Aunt Jeannie. Everyone's attention was at the tip of a needle as she went and talked to him. When she returned, we asked her what was the matter. She said, "The Pakistani troops have surrendered."

Our hearts danced with joy, but we could not express it as the enemy soldiers were still in Chittagong and also a few miles ahead of us.

Then at seven o'clock on two radios, one was Uncle Minich's and the other Aunt Jeannie's, we heard news after news! Speeches from India. Yes, the Pakistani troops had surrendered.

Uncle Minich got a Bangladesh flag and placed it on the dining room table. I think for the first place in Chittagong victory seemed to be only in this house.

Then on December 17 the Indian soldiers came through Chittagong. It was like a volcano which remains dormant for a long time before it gathers sufficient energy to begin eruption! Everywhere Bangladesh flags were flown and people shouted, "Joi Bangla!"—the only language of 70,000,000 souls for the first time after nine months of struggle.

It was a time of sorrow; it was a season of sacrifice; it was a period of struggle. The golden Bangladesh dazzled like the twinkling stars in the moonlit night—the calm after a storm of brutality and hostility. Seventy million lives are now relieved —no more horrible sights.

We mourn the death of countless young lives, brave and bold, who chose bullets rather than slavery. Bengali youths were dragged from their peaceful world of songs and poems and thrown out into the arena of modern warfare. But they rose up quickly to the situation. We pay our deepest respect for those sons of our golden motherland who fought against tyranny, atrocity, and oppression.

Now we wait for the dreams to materialize.

**All here and
accounted for**

14

All here and accounted for

And then it was Christmas.

With our new freedom we went from house to house rejoicing, singing, praying, and drinking tea. One of the homes where we were especially welcomed was that of the family whose father had been spared by the military because "a foreign sahib had come looking for him."

How many lived to enjoy that Christmas because the Lord had permitted His servants to be in this place at this time? I wonder—

We could enjoy our own Christmas all the more.

No ships had come in bearing love-filled gifts from home, for the harbor was jammed with sunken ships. Even the Christmas cards didn't arrive until the following May.

It was enough that we were all alive. And we did have a Merry Christmas.

There was scarcely a dry eye among the congregation gathered under a canvas awning that Christmas Sunday. The crowd was so large that we had to move out of our meeting room onto the back lawn.

John Sircar started his message with: "We never thought we would have a Christmas this year. We did not know if we would be alive . . . ."

But we were all there:

— Reid, Lynn returned from Malumghat, and myself
— Khoka Sen with his wife and family

— The Nundy family, with Mr. Nundy still weak from his recent illness

— Menindro's family and with them the Hindus whose daughters they had saved

— The twenty-one Christians who had lived for months at the Bible Information Center

— Mr. & Mrs. Rodgers and the two little girls

— Drs. Peter and Reba MacField and little "Bubbly"

— Lucy's family with the little brother born in the midst of the trouble

— All the Boshus and dear Didi-Ma

— The nurses and their brothers returned from shelter in the tribal villages around the Baptist Mission Hospital, Chandraghona

— Babla and Stephen dressed in their Mukti Bahini uniforms

John's message was about freedom; he told of the reality of peace and the joy of knowing the Prince of Peace. He told us things that he hadn't mentioned before.

"How blessed we have been to see God directly guide us by His almighty loving Hand! People all over the world have heard of the atrocities committed in Bangladesh. Killing, looting, raping have become incidental matters. Many people left their homes to take shelter in India or in remote villages.

"At first some Hindus and Muslims as well as Christians came here to the Bible Information Center for refuge, but most of the former group left to seek a safer, more interior place. At one time we had fifty-one people living here.

"Each night I used to spend some time in prayer with the sheltered people. I told them that we in ourselves have no power, no strength, no knowledge, no wisdom—nothing. But God is with us.

"During the first week in April we were always hearing sounds of firing from all directions. Mills and factories were burning. One day, just at noon, the firing started from both sides. The Pak soldiers were on the road behind us with heavy weapons. The East Bengal Regiment were in houses on the road in front of us. We were in the middle. There was continuous fighting until 3:15—not a single minute without a shot. Rifles, machine guns, and other weapons shot their ammunition through the air. When a mortar landed only fifteen yards from the building, I thought the roof of the house was gone. The place shook as if it were an earthquake. As a result, all of the windows were smashed. A bullet blasted through our signboard and entered the building. Shells spattered thousands of holes in our boundary wall, but no one was hurt.

"We were all lying on the floor; some of the women fainted from fear. I was also afraid. I thought, *Now they will come and kill us.*

"The Pakistan soldiers were on top of a nearby building using binoculars to spy in all directions. We put screens in all the window openings so that they could not see us. Some of us peeked out from around the edge of the screen. . We saw them turn their binoculars in our direction. We were sure they would come that night and kill us. Feeling that this would be my last day in the world, I wrote letters to my widowed mother, the rest of my family, my friends, the members of the church. I asked them to forgive me if I had done anything wrong.

"Everyone in the house was so afraid they began to cry. Then faith came to my mind. I called the people together and said, 'Do you believe in prayer?'

"'Oh yes,' they answered.

"'Then let me pray.'

"That twilight I cried and prayed. 'Oh Jesus, hear our prayer and save us from death.' Then I continued, 'Lord Jesus, I do not expect to hear the sound of *any* firing around us tonight.'

"Do you know what happened that night? Not one of us in that building heard a thing. Do you think that the firing around us had stopped? Certainly not; heavy fighting continued throughout the night. But in the morning each one of us remarked that we had passed a quiet night. No one heard any noise at all!

"In the morning eight army men came, equipped with machine guns, wireless sets, and heavy weapons. As they entered by the back door, everyone became very frightened. Women and children ran to me crying, 'The army has come.'

"I decided that I would speak to them in a courteous manner. I stood up, and taking three Bibles—one in English, one in Bengali, and one in Urdu, their mother tongue (My idea was to prove that we are Christians.) — I stepped out to greet them. 'Good morning. How are you?' I said and extended my hand for a handshake.

"The leader looked at me and shouted, 'Stop!' So I stood up straight like a statue while he held his machine gun just inches from my chest. Two other men held their machine guns two yards from me, one on the right and one on the left. Death was certain. My only thought at the moment was, *How many bullets will pass through me if they all pull the triggers?*

"Then they started asking questions, 'Are there any of the Mukti Bahini around here? Has there been any firing from this office? Do you know where the Bengal Regiment is holed up? Who are these people in this building?'

"I answered, 'I am a Christian. These are my people.'

"I told them that they were free to search the office because I knew there was nothing there; we were innocent. They went from room to room. There is a small storeroom which was locked. They ordered it opened. There were some phonographs in the storeroom. They started to take some away. I did not want them destroying our equipment, but I thought that if I said they could not take them, they would beat and kill me, so I said, 'All right, if you want to take those things, I have no objection myself, but you will fall into trouble because this is American property.' They did not take the record players.

"The Pakistan military always had suspicious minds. When they were leaving the office, they walked backwards, holding the machine guns on us, and called out, 'If we hear any sound from this building, we will shoot you all without any investigation.'

"God gave me strength. I stepped up to them and told them to go away. If they wanted to fight in a religious place, they could go to their own mosque, but they were not going to fight in our church. I followed them to the gate and shut it behind them.

"To the glory of God we can say that throughout all of the horror and trouble that we have seen, not one of our national believers has been killed. God gave me this verse which has been my strength and stay. 'A thousand shall fall at thy side, and ten thousand at thy right hand; but it shall not come nigh thee' (Psalm 91:7)."

We rose to sing a favorite Bengali Christmas carol:

> Raise the flag singing "Victory to Jesus"
> Everyone sing it together today.

> In the sky of Bethlehem the sun of righteousness has risen
> By its light the wise men awake.

> The Loving Father sent His Son
> And there will be peace and love in the world.

> Praise to the Son, the remover of our sins
> Raising both hands, sing "Victory to Jesus!"

Joi Bangla! Victory to Bengal!
Joi Jesu! Victory to Jesus!